P9-DGF-012

OUR
SAGES,
GOD,
AND ISRAEL

Talmud Yerushalmi. English. Selections.

OUR
SAGES,
GOD,
AND ISRAEL ;

BM
516
.T282
E 45

An Anthology of the
Talmud of the Land of Israel

Jacob Neusner

Chappaqua, New York

© Copyright 1984 by Jacob Neusner
Translations © 1982, 1983, 1984
by The University of Chicago.
All rights reserved.

Library of Congress Cataloging in Publication Data
Talmud Yerushalmi. English. Selections.

Our sages, God, and Israel.
Includes index.
1. Aggada—Translations into English. I. Neusner, Jacob,
1932-   . II. Title.
BM516.T282E5   1984   296.1'2405   84-23793
ISBN 0-940646-18-8

Textual translations are adapted from The Talmud of the Land
of Israel: A Preliminary Translation and Explanation *and
appear by special arrangement with The University of Chicago
Press. No part of this book may be reproduced or transmitted
in any form or by any means, electronic or mechanical, including photocopying, recording, or any information storage or
retrieval system without written permission from Rossel Books
and The University of Chicago.*

Published by Rossel Books
44 Dunbow Drive
Chappaqua, New York 10514
(914) 238-8954

For

Louis Newman
Roger Brooks
Howard Schwartz
Judith Romney Wegner
Paul Flesher

A memento of what we did together
in creating something out of nothing.

1982-1983

I remember the devotion of your youth . . .
how you followed me in the wilderness
in a land not sown.

Contents

OUR
SAGES,
GOD,
AND ISRAEL

Preface

AN ANTHOLOGY OF THE Talmud of the Land of Israel, also known as the *Yerushalmi* or the Palestinian Talmud, raises some simple questions. What is the Talmud? What is the particular Talmud at hand? Why is it important?

The answers begin at Sinai, so Judaism has always taught. When God revealed the Torah to Moses at Mount Sinai, God handed on revelation in two forms. One form was in writing. The written Torah reaches us as the Scriptures, the Hebrew Bible. The other form was oral. That is to say, part of "the one whole Torah of Moses, our rabbi," came not in writing but orally to Moses, and from him to the prophets and sages. This part of the Torah was memorized and handed on by word of mouth; hence it was called the "oral Torah." So the "one whole Torah" of Judaism comes to us in two separate media, written and oral.

This fundamental conviction is important to this anthology of the Yerushalmi because, at a later time, centuries after Sinai, the oral part of the Torah did reach written form. Specifically, it was in the document called the Mishnah — a great philosophical law code compiled ca. 200 C.E., credited to the sponsorship of Rabbi Judah the

Patriarch. The Mishnah demanded close and careful study. The great sages of two Jewish communities of the early centuries C.E. — the settlements in the Land of Israel and in Babylonia — received the Mishnah and explained its meaning and application. What they discovered about the meaning of this written version of the oral Torah also eventually reached written form. In writing, the vast expansion and explanation of the Mishnah produced in Babylonia was called the Babylonian Talmud, and the equivalent treatment accomplished in the Land of Israel (based on the very same Mishnah) became the Yerushalmi, the Jerusalem Talmud (alternately known either as the Talmud of the Land of Israel or the Palestinian Talmud).

The work of compiling the Yerushalmi was accomplished in two stages. The first was a systematic account of the civil law, in the tractates Baba Qamma, Baba Mesia, and Baba Batra. This part of the Yerushalmi reached its final form in Caesarea, in the Land of Israel, ca. 350 C.E. The remainder was concluded, it is generally thought, about a half-century later, ca. 400 C.E. (The equivalent work for the Babylonian Talmud came about a century later.)

Independently, the two Talmuds provide a commentary upon a single text — namely, the Mishnah. They take up a common task. But the sages of each community carry on the work in their own way. Hence (1) we define "the Talmud" as a set of two systematic commentaries to the Mishnah, the one produced in the Land of Israel, the other in Babylonia. The particular Talmud at hand, (2) the Yerushalmi, is the systematic explanation of the Mishnah created among the circles of sages of the Land of Israel (mainly in Tiberias, Sepphoris, and Caesarea) in the third and fourth centuries C.E. The Talmud of the Land of Israel, or Yerushalmi, is important (3) because, in principle, it forms part of the Torah revealed to Moses at Sinai. Specifically, it carries forward the explanation and application of the oral portion of "the one whole Torah of Moses, our rabbi."

The reason that our sages of the Land of Israel found it important to study and amplify the Mishnah is simple. They served as officials of the autonomous Jewish government of what the Jews call the Land of Israel and the Romans called "Palestine" (hence, the Yerushalmi is sometimes referred to as the "Palestinian"

Talmud). The Jews in the Land of Israel followed their own laws, administered by their own government. At the time of the closure of the Mishnah, that government was headed by Rabbi Judah the Patriarch. For two centuries thereafter, it was in the hands of his heirs. The Romans, for their part, permitted the Jews to take charge of a great many matters that seemed to Rome to make no significant difference. Our sages, then, adopted the Mishnah as the source of law for their government, and they applied it as the recognized and official law code for the Jewish nation in its land.

Accordingly, when we enter the pages of the Talmud of the Land of Israel, we find ourselves in the midst of a lively, self-governing nation, part of a still larger empire but essentially autonomous and semi-independent. That favorable situation prevailed through the later second, third, and fourth centuries. At the beginning of the fifth century, times changed for the worse, and the political institution on which our Talmud rested came to an end.

The same benign circumstances – Jewish self-government in a large and loose imperial system – prevailed in Babylonia, which formed part of the western frontier of the vast Iranian empire of that time. In fact, the Jews lived under still more favorable conditions in Babylonia (present-day Iraq) than in Roman "Palestine."

The two Talmuds come to us as gifts of Jews who explored the meaning of nationhood, who sought to create a kingdom of priests and a holy people. The specific issue confronted by both Talmuds is how Jews might live as an autonomous nation by the law of Torah. The two Talmuds describe a Jewish world for which, from their time to ours, Jews would long – an age in which Jews were free to obey the laws of Torah and live by their principles. The Talmuds supply a model for ways of thinking about the Torah when Jews enjoy the freedom and opportunity to take seriously and in very practical terms its principles and teachings.

The Talmud of Babylonia came from a community living outside its own land, whereas the Yerushalmi derived from a community that lived by right – by God's determination – in its own Holy Land. That may be one reason that the Jews of the Diaspora for centuries after the completion of the Babylonian Talmud concentrated attention on that Talmud. This led to the virtual neglect of the Yerushalmi. Only in the modern age, with the return of Jews to the Land of Israel, did the study of the Talmud of the Land of Israel get under way in a systematic manner. Accordingly, the Yerushalmi survived essentially unknown among the great masters of Torah learning.

THE TRANSLATION

When I undertook to translate the Yerushalmi into English, therefore, my intention was to make the text available to an English-speaking world long closed off from it. My translation is contained in thirty-five volumes, under the title *The Talmud of the Land of Israel, A Preliminary Translation and Explanation* (Chicago: The University of Chicago Press, 1982-1988). As of this writing, volumes 27-35 are in print, and the remainder will come through the press at the rate of five per year. Ten of the thirty-five volumes (I-VIII, XII, XVI) will be produced by my former students and a colleague. I call the translation "preliminary" because many problems remain unsolved by me. These are of three kinds:

First, we have no first-rate version of the Hebrew and Aramaic text. The available printed text contains many errors. Worse still, no one has yet brought together all the evidence of the way the text existed in the centuries after it reached closure.

Second, we have no first-rate dictionary to tell us the meaning of many strange words. While much progress has been made in the study of the Hebrew of our sages as well as the Aramaic used by them in the Land of Israel, no dictionary offers the up-to-date results of modern learning. The only available dictionary is close to a century old.

Third, we have no modern explanation of the meaning of passages. The Talmud at hand, like its Babylonian counterpart, is abbreviated and presents its ideas in elliptical language. Therefore, we have to supply not only words equivalent to what is in the Hebrew and Aramaic, but also sentences that complete or make sense of the text.

Translating a text such as this is not like translating one that is lucid and fully exposed in its own language. Rather, to translate the Yerushalmi is to supply a commentary; in the nature of things, that means we have to rely upon the great learned commentaries of past masters of the text. Only two complete commentaries of the Yerushalmi exist, and there is room for many more. ´

Consequently, my translation serves as only a first step toward a full and reliable account of the Yerushalmi. But it is a solid step forward, and I estimate that approximately 90 percent of the whole will stand the test of time.

THE WORK AT HAND

This anthology is a selection of passages of the Yerushalmi for a wide audience. All passages here seem to me to rest upon a good text, valid explanations of the meaning of passages, correct interpretations of the sense of the words. I have omitted passages that seemed to present problems calling for further study.

Why is it important to offer this anthology? Precisely because the Yerushalmi is not well known. The Yerushalmi has been mainly inaccessible to most of us. The Babylonian Talmud, by contrast, has been known in both German and English for some time.

Further, the writings at hand bear an important message to today's world. They speak of holiness and salvation, addressing a people demoralized and in defeat. Basing their discussions on the Mishnah, the Yerushalmi's writers faced a world much like the one Jews would continue to confront until nearly our own day. No longer a recognized nation, the Jews lived on past glory and future hope. Cherishing the holy Torah, the Jews faced in Christianity a dominant power that claimed that same Torah, yet read it very differently. The teachings of our sages of the Yerushalmi, as much as those now found in the other Talmud, the *Bavli* or Babylonian Talmud, for that long span of time would define Judaism and sustain the Jewish people. And they still do. So an anthology of formerly inaccessible teachings about the critical issues of Jewish existence surely provides an invaluable treasure for a community that needs sustenance wherever it is available.

A society and community "in our image, after our likeness"– that is what Israel, the Jewish people, is called to create. The Yerushalmi presents a vast and systematic account of what

Jews are supposed to do in order to constitute "a kingdom of priests and a holy people," a community formed and framed in God's image of humanity. The authors of the Yerushalmi, taking up the Mishnah, brought to full realization in everyday life that ancient vision of Israel's prophets and sages. They tell in detail how to live life in accord with the Torah. For this book I have selected from their writings passages that, laid out in accord with what I conceive to be the basic issues of Israel's public life as they unfold, tell us the message at hand: how to conduct the affairs of society in God's image.

Three actors are presented here: Israel, God, and the sage. Of the three, it is the sage – the master who in the here-and-now teaches us what the Torah requires so we may conform to God's image and likeness for us – who is at the center. The sage ("our sages, of blessed memory") forms the focus of the Yerushalmi as of many other writings of the ancient rabbis. Israel's condition in this world, God's condition in this world – both come to full and complete expression in the sage.

My story in this anthology is in two parts. First, in Chapters 1-5, comes the crisis of the world, for the individual in death, for Israel in exile, and for God in the age of unredemption. Second, in Chapters 6-10, comes the resolution of the crisis in the persons of "our sages," who stand for humanity in God's image and set the standard for the society of Israel.

THE SETTING

This anthology is a handbook on how one group of intellectuals represented its theory of humanity: who we are, where we are heading, and why. The Talmud of the Land of Israel presents a systematic account of how its authors think an entire nation and society, the Jewish people living in the Holy Land in the third and fourth centuries of the common or Christian era, should imagine and construct the world. The Talmud portrays the imagination of a handful of sages, an estate of men (no women then) who qualify as community officials through their knowledge of Scripture and associated tradition. This world constructed in the mind deserves our attention for a number of reasons, but demands it for only one. The sages' construction of reality provides a fully spelled-out example of how, in mind and through intellect, people propose to solve this-worldly, concrete problems of a quite relevant order. Lacking power, claiming to govern only an unimportant and defeated people, having to sort out the distasteful possibilities presented by the condition of weakness in contrast with the illusion of consequence, the sages at hand left us a stunning model. It is an instance, with few parallels, of humanity's capacity, through an act of will, to overcome and endure.

The intellect—in God's image—in the view of the Yerushalmi, brings to full exposure the governing force of will and human determination. In joining the stout heart to the rigorous mind, the Talmud's sages demonstrated, for all to see, that emotion tamed by criticism, the will shaped by the mind, together constitute the one force able to endure and transcend all things. Used as we are to distinguish heart from mind, emotion from intellect, we confront in the Yerushalmi, and in the sages who wrote it, a challenge to our firmest convictions about what is self-evident. That is why we cannot evade the matter at hand, the theory of humanity, the image and view of ourselves as sentient and yet thinking beings, with which the Talmud defines our present and settled sense of self: all heart or all mind.

We may gain access to that image of humanity in three ways, of which this book represents the third and simplest. The first is the complete preliminary translation. The second is through literary and religious-historical studies of the Yerushalmi. These I offered in *The Talmud of the Land of Israel. 35. Introduction. Taxonomy*, and in *Judaism in Society: The Evidence of the Yerushalmi* (Chicago: The University of Chicago Press, 1983). The former presents an inductive theory of definition of the Talmud at hand; the latter offers a systematic account, from outside to inside, of the Talmud's system as a whole, context, text, and matrix.

This third way, the anthology of selected materials, allows the sages of the Yerushalmi to speak in their own words but on issues of concern to ourselves as much as to them. Here, therefore, I will try to show how the Yerushalmi portrays humanity: its image of the world. We shall work our way inductively through a sequence of sources I have translated and chosen as evocative and revealing. This is how they speak; this is what they have to say.

A BRIEF SUMMARY

While I have dealt at length with the content of the Yerushalmi and its method in the volumes cited above, let me summarize the findings by way of introduction to this anthology.

What is the Talmud of the Land of Israel? The Yerushalmi is a systematic commentary on the Mishnah of Rabbi Judah the Patriarch, the philosophic law code composed ca. 200 C.E., prescribing modes of sanctification of Israel's life. A remarkably limited repertoire of exegetical initiatives was available to the framers of the Yerushalmi's discussions of the Mishnah. They usually chose and carried out one of a handful of procedures. Essentially, these may be reduced to two: to explain the simple meaning of a passage; to expand and theorize about one passage in the light of other passages (or of a problem common to several passages). Exegesis, therefore, may take the form of exposition of the meaning, or expansion upon the meaning, of a given pericope of the Mishnah. It follows that if we understand what the Talmud does with a single item, we may confidently claim to describe and make sense of what the Talmud is apt to do with a great many such items.

In this book I rarely give an example of how the sages of the Yerushalmi explain the meaning of a passage of the Mishnah. Most of that exegetical work pertains to the exposition of ideas not particular to the sages of the Talmud by definition. While the sages' modes of thought are their own, the exegetical problems come down to them from an earlier generation. Most of what they say represents a series of choices dictated by other people's logic. So when we recognize that the Talmud of the Land of Israel constitutes, in form and in the bulk of its substance, an exegetical exercise serving the Mishnah, we realize, too, that the materials in this book do not represent the rhetoric and discourse of the larger document. They are tangential, at best, to Mishnah exegesis.

They are central, however, to any consideration of the image of humanity portrayed in the document as a whole. For when the masters raise their eyes from the Mishnah in particular, to look outward at the world of Israel at large, they speak in general terms and about readily identifiable human issues. What they have to say, to be sure, emerges from deep reflection on the particulars of the Mishnah and, of course, of Scripture. But the modes of discourse paramount in this anthology do not characterize the bulk of the literature from which the items have been chosen. So, in all, the Yerushalmi is mostly an exegetical work, supplying also discursive units of thought, and it is the latter that predominate here.

What is the Talmud about? I answer this question in *Judaism in Society: The Evidence of the Yerushalmi*, and a brief reprise of the method of that book will suffice here. In that book I seek first (Chapter 1) to place the Yerushalmi within its larger context in the Roman world. Then (Chapter 2), I ask where the document is to be located in the history of the Jewish people and in relation to other works of the larger Judaism of which it forms part. I propose, third, to describe the principal points of insistence, the things on which the document lays emphasis throughout its entire inquiry, in all of its exegetical initiatives (Chapter 3). These two matters — external setting in Judaism and internal context of discourse — define the Yerushalmi's particular and distinctive characteristics. Turning outward to the matrix, that larger framework in which the text is located — that is, other writings by the same sort of Judaic authorities, rabbis — I propose, fourth, to describe what the text at hand tells us about its own sponsors, its picture of the social role of the particular kind of figure who speaks both here and in other books of the same place, time, and type of Judaism (Chapter 4). That seems to me the necessary first step in comparing the document to other documents — that is, to discover what it has in common with other documents of its type belonging to the same subdivision of its larger classification. I then, fifth, try to point to the purpose of the document, the message put forward by this text, in the name of its authorities, for the larger world of Judaism (Chapter 5). Here I ask about the points on which the Yerushalmi's · framers insist, and why what they say matters.

Accordingly, description proceeds from context to text to matrix. The opening part presents the question of the book, the relationship of the document to its age. The answers are adduced, first, inductively, through a close reading of the recurrent traits of the text itself; second, not altogether deductively, through an account of those traits of the text congruent to traits of other rabbinic texts of the same class. What are the results? The questions posed at the end of Chapter 1 of *Judaism in Society: The Evidence of the Yerushalmi* are answered in the repertoire of extracts of the next four chapters: a reasoned, uniform discourse (Chapter 2) yielding (1) certainty about God's will (Chapter 3), (2) authority for the rabbi (Chapter 4), and, (3) salvation for Israel (Chapter 5). Given the calamities of the late fourth and early fifth centuries, in which the Yerushalmi came into being, and the uncertainty about what was to follow, we shall hardly be surprised to discover a document aimed — as this anthology shows — on every page at reaffirming and validating the faith of Judaism as the rabbis had framed it.

In an age of deep self-doubt, the Yerushalmi's framers spoke confidently about the basis, in revelation accurately transmitted and logically understood, of Israel's true salvation through the Torah as the rabbis represented it. That is the meaning of the Yerushalmi's Judaism, deriving from its context, the traits of its text, and its larger matrix.

This rapid summary of the results of my efforts to define the document and to describe its principal points of emphasis places the present anthology into context. In the Introduction I explain in greater detail the human situation of the framers of the document and how I think we should read their mode of addressing that situation. For at every turn, in each story and saying, we find a statement that encompasses the whole. Context dictates content, so that the world that people must endure governs the issues they choose to confront. Accordingly, if we wish to understand the vision of humanity captured in the massive text of the Yerushalmi, we do well to work from the known to the unknown, from the condition of Israel to the minds of the sages of Israel.

The dedication of this book speaks for itself. I express thanks to David Altshuler of George Washington University, who gave me the idea of making such an anthology and to the students to whom the book is dedicated for reading it and giving me their suggestions for improvement. Judith Romney Wegner edited the entire manuscript.

J.N.
Passover, 5743
Providence, Rhode Island

Introduction

THE TALMUD OF THE LAND OF ISRAEL rests upon the Mishnah, a vast statement of law brought to closure about 200 C.E. Serving as an elaborate explanation and amplification of the Mishnah, the Yerushalmi – the Talmud of the Land of Israel – was worked out over two hundred years and completed about 400 C.E. Thus it presents the appearance of an ongoing and unending construction – continually growing and changing in the course of time. But the Yerushalmi is not aimless. Rather, it is like a cathedral on which for generation after generation people lavished their piety, wealth, and talent. Exhibiting striking differences in matters of detail, the final construction even after centuries creates an impression of remarkable unity and coherence. So it is with the Yerushalmi.

The Mishnah, for its part, contains ideas that probably go back to the early part of the first century. As a basic codification of Jewish law, the Mishnah furthermore draws extensively on Hebrew Scriptures of well over a millennium before its time. The Talmud, taking over the Mishnah and reshaping it in accordance with the needs and tastes of the generations of continuators, carried forth this same labor along a single, if not straight, line of development.

THE MISHNAH AND
THE TALMUD

In this anthology, we deal only with the end-product, the Yerushalmi in its final expression. The Talmud at hand testifies to a remarkably coherent viewpoint. It is the viewpoint of its ultimate authors: the sages of the Land of Israel who memorized the Mishnah and applied some of its laws in their work as officials of the Jewish autonomous government of Roman Palestine. These authors were among the most influential writers of antiquity. How so? The results of their writing, which we know as "Judaism," remained authoritative and normative from their day onward. Accordingly, the worldview and way of life, the "Judaism," to which the Yerushalmi testifies forms one plank in the bridge that leads from antiquity to the beginning of the Middle Ages, from the Middle East to Europe, from the end of the classical age to the nascent moment of our own time and place.

About 200 C.E., the Mishnah, on which the Yerushalmi rests, looks back to classical times. It describes a utopia, an orderly world, in which Israelite society is neatly divided among its castes, arranged in priority around the center that is the Temple, systematically engaged in a life of sanctification, remote from the disorderly events of the day. Such a world existed only in the imagination of the Mishnah's authors. The Talmud, about 400 C.E., portrays the chaos of Jews living among gentiles, governed by a diversity of authorities, lacking all order and arrangement, awaiting a time of salvation for which, through sanctification, they prepare themselves. That vision conforms to the everyday reality of the age.

The Mishnah's imaginary Israel is governed by an Israelite king, a high priest, and a Sanhedrin. The Talmud's flesh-and-blood Jews lived under rabbis near at hand, who settled everyday disputes of streets and households, and, further under distant archons of a nameless state, to be manipulated and placated on earth as in Heaven. The Mishnah's Judaism breathes the pure air of public piazza and stoa; the Talmud's, the ripe stench of private alleyway and courtyard.

The image of the Mishnah's Judaism is comparable to the majestic Parthenon, perfect in all its proportions, conceived in a single moment of pure rationality. The Talmud's Judaism is an inchoate cathedral in process, the labor of many generations, each of its parts the conception of a diverse moment of devotion, all of them the culmination of an ongoing and evolving revelation in the here and now, a snare for Heaven's light. The Mishnah is a noble theory of it all, Judaism's counterpart to Plato's *Republic* and Aristotle's *Politics*. To the Talmud, classical antiquity supplies no analogy.

So when we study the Mishnah, we contemplate a fine conception of nowhere in particular, addressed to whom it may concern. When we turn to the Yerushalmi, we see a familiar world, as we have known it from the Talmud's day to our own. We perceive something of our own day, studying a Judaism much like our own. Essentially, the Mishnah marks the end of the ancient and Middle Eastern, the Yerushalmi the beginning of the modern and Western (as well as Middle Eastern) epoch in the history of Judaism.

THE AGE OF THE TALMUD

The period covered by the texts in this anthology is marked off, at the beginning, by the completion of the Mishnah, about 200 C.E., and, at the end, by the closure of the Talmud of the Land of Israel, about 400 C.E. These tumultuous centuries witnessed the transition in world history from late antiquity to early medieval times. The Roman Empire became two, dividing East from West, and turned from pagan to Christian, from the mode of being we know as classical to the one we identify as medieval. The birth of Judaism thus forms a chapter in the history of the movement of the West from its Greek, Roman, and Israelite beginnings to its full expression in Christianity for the generality of Europe; (later on) in Islam for Africa and Asia; and in Judaism for the margins of both worlds. True, the birth of Judaism in context fills little more than a paragraph out of the long chapter of the movement from classical to medieval and hence modern civilization, both East and West. But it is a suggestive chapter, exemplifying in its accessibility much that otherwise lies beyond our capacity for detailed description and explanation, the social world of village and private life. In what is small, we may discern large things; in detail, the configuration of the whole.

THE LITERARY HISTORY: FROM THE MISHNAH TO THE TALMUD

Let us now define what changes. What marks the turning of the way? The shift is evoked, in literary terms, in the transition from the Mishnah to the Talmud of the Land of Israel. From the strict and formal classicism of the Mishnah—like Plato's *Republic,* describing for no one in particular an ideal society nowhere to be found—the Judaism described by the Talmud of the Land of Israel turned to the disorderly detail of the workaday world. If Aristotle's *Politics* had been written as a gloss to Plato's *Republic,* amplifying and extending piece by piece the once whole and coherent writing of Plato, we should have a rough analogy to what the Talmud does for the Mishnah of Rabbi Judah the Patriarch. If, further, many philosophers had taken up the fantastic account of the *Republic* and, out of its materials and other writings, worked out new *Republic*s, bringing diversity to what had been a single conception and cogent book, we should have a usable precedent for what happened from 200 to 400 C.E. in the move, in Judaism, from the ancient to the medieval mode: from theoretical to practical, monothetic to polythetic, uniform to diverse, cogent to chaotic, and system to incremental tradition.

Before us is the rich literary context of the Yerushalmi. The second century yielded a single document of the evolving Judaism—the Mishnah. The dawn of the fifth century witnessed the beginning and formation of many variants and the completion of one authoritative version. The Tosefta, a supplement to the Mishnah's materials in the Mishnah's own idiom and structure, was taking shape. The Sifra, a compilation of exegesis pertinent to Leviticus, with special interest in the relationship of the Mishnah's laws to those of Leviticus, would soon follow. By that time, the Talmud of the Land of Israel, a vast amplification of the Mishnah, neared closure. In the hundred years beyond the closure of the Yerushalmi, a quite different mode of collection and organization of sayings, represented by the compilations of exegetical remarks on Genesis and Leviticus, called Genesis Rabbah and Leviticus Rabbah, would come to full expression. Nor may we ignore the other, greater and more influential, Talmud, the one created in Babylonia, generally thought to have reached its final form in the two centuries after the Yerushalmi's closure.

Accordingly, the Mishnah, a single document, stands at the head of many paths. Numerous roads lead onward from the Mishnah. But none leads backward from it, save the leaps to Sinai conveyed in the prooftexts of Scripture cited by the sages of the Mishnah and Talmud. Among these paths onward from the Mishnah, the Yerushalmi and the Babylonian Talmuds and Midrash collections mark the principal road.

The Yerushalmi, the Talmud of the Land of Israel, testifies to the existence of a coherent worldview and way of life embodied in a distinctive society, that of the sages or rabbis – masters and disciples – of the third and fourth centuries in the Land of Israel. The present anthology illustrates many of the principal traits of that worldview and its way of life. But, I must emphasize, the Yerushalmi is no complete system of Judaism contained in a single document. This fact presents a contrast to the Mishnah.

The Mishnah lays forth a six-part system, dealing with (1) sanctification of the Temple and the Holy Land, (2) the holy-day life of the people and of (3) its family life and (4) civil affairs, (5) the conduct of the agricultural economy, and (6) the celebration of the natural year. Each element of the encompassing life of the Jewish people in the natural world is brought into correspondence with its counterpart in the supernatural world. Thus the Mishnah presents a full picture of the ideal world of holy Israel, stating in connection with each detail what it wishes to say about the whole.

Whereas all that we know about the Mishnah's system is in the law code itself, the Yerushalmi is quite different. The Judaism to which the Yerushalmi testifies defines the matrix in which, among other documents, the Yerushalmi came into being. But the Yerushalmi does not constitute the sole, or the one important, corpus of evidence about that kind of Judaism. Nor is there any single document that expresses that whole. Accordingly, the Judaism in the Talmud of the Land of Israel is not the Judaism of that book alone, in the same way as the Judaism to which the Mishnah testifies is expressed within the Mishnah, whole and complete.

This is my main point. While the Mishnah exhaustively answers any and all questions about its Judaism, the Yerushalmi, answering many questions about the Judaism represented in its pages, is by no means the sole source of answers. Numerous questions addressed by the Judaism of the Yerushalmi are answered – in the same or similar ways – in other documents altogether. The evidence of the Yerushalmi about the Judaism attested in its pages must be described in a way quite different from the way in which we lay out evidence of the Mishnah about the Judaism expressed within the Mishnah. One gives evidence of a world beyond itself, a world of which it is an important component. The other gives evidence only about itself and the worldview contemplated within its words.

From the literary setting of the Talmud of the Land of Israel, we turn to the historical one. What was the Land of Israel in the period at hand, and what conditions governed the human issues distinctive to the time, place, and people for which the Yerushalmi speaks?

THE LAND OF ISRAEL WITHIN THE ROMAN EMPIRE

The Talmud stresses the themes of certainty, consensus, and authority. These points of insistence also express a general concern: to overcome doubt, confusion, diversity, and civil chaos. When we look up from the Talmud's pages to the time and place in which they were written, we should not be surprised to discover that at the same time – the late fourth century – the world was emerging from an age of disorder. After a half-century of disaster, the old order had given way to a new one.

What had happened, in brief summary, was this: at the beginning of the third century, the centuries-old principate, under which the Roman Empire had flourished, came to an end. For two hundred and fifty years, the Augustan political structure had sustained a vast empire in peace and consequent prosperity. From 235 to 285, by contrast, the government fell apart in civil wars. From the murder of Alexander Severus in 235 to the victory of Diocletian in 284, anarchy prevailed. The twenty years of peace provided by Diocletian from 285 to 305 were followed by further civil war. It was Constantine who in the early fourth century reunited the Empire and reestablished government. The causes of collapse and ruin need not detain us. What is important to know is that, for the world at large, the fourth century was a time of reordering and reconstruction of stability. Establishing his capital in the East, at Byzantium, Constantine rebuilt a sizable administration, capable of raising money to pay for an army and support a bureaucracy.

To state matters simply, the third century produced collapse; the fourth century, reconstruction. In the third century the old order crumbled. In the fourth, the rubble of the classical age was reshaped into the foundations of the medieval world. The classical world of 200 C.E. stood continuous with a long and stable past. The incipient medieval age of 400 C.E. looked forward to a long and continuous future, with institutions stretching onward to Europe and the Middle Ages. The Eastern empire was so strongly founded that it endured for another thousand years. But in between, and behind, and near at hand, in the interim, one could see only the abyss – a long past, an uncertain future, a difficult present.

The frontiers of the Roman Empire cracked open in the middle of the third century, admitting armies of marauders from the east, north, and west. The task of the later third and fourth century emperors, both Eastern and Western, was to stem the tide, reconstruct a defensible border, and reestablish effective government over vast territories. This they did in ample measure in the East. So the history of the Land of Israel as part of the Roman Empire of the third and fourth centuries is the story of crisis and remission, calamitous collapse, and painful reconstruction. While the Empire suffered assault on all fronts, a long sequence of hapless emperors proved unable to protect the homeland and defend the frontiers. The Empire was saved, toward the second half of the third century, by a military revolution. The revolution threw back the barbarians at the Danube in 269, in the eastern provinces in 273, and on the Iranian front in 296. The army then produced the talent required to reorganize the government itself. Sons of freedmen, cattle herders and pig farmers in the countryside, rose to power and reestablished the Empire that the old aristocracy had been unable to save. An aristocracy of service, in the time of Constantine, from 324 to 337, completed the restoration of the civil service and bureaucracy, so government once more became possible. All of this happened at the surface. Underneath, the old established order continued its slow, majestic progress. The latent or subterranean history, to a corner of which the Yerushalmi testifies, was considerably less dramatic but no less important.

THE LAND OF ISRAEL AS A STATE OF MIND

From a political standpoint, it is difficult to say there actually was a "Land of Israel." In the period of which we speak, Jews lived in and under multiple polities, of which their own ethnarchy was only one. The ethnarch, called *nasi,* or patriarch, ruled the Jews of the Land of Israel from the second century until the beginning of the fifth. The rabbis served as his clerks and bureaucrats, and the Mishnah served as his constitution and code. A map of Jewish settlement in the territories imagined by the Talmud to constitute the "Land of Israel," marking each town with a color appropriate to its ethnic majority, would appear speckled. The Jewish government controlled persons, not territory. The Jewish points on the map would call to mind not the evenly spaced spots of a leopard, nor the stripes of a zebra, but the blotches of the English springer spaniel. Some heavy concentrations remained in the Galilee, on the one side, and in the region called "the South," around present-day Lod, on the other.

Such was the Land of Israel as a geographical and political realm. Accordingly, geographical definitions bore little resemblance to the concrete reality. The "Land of Israel" was a state of mind. How so? The "Land" was nowhere in particular. Rather, it was scattered throughout the countryside. There was no Jewish sovereignty in any single contiguous area. Rather, there was much authority exercised here and there. No wonder that the Talmud's rabbis, like others in the Jewish world, in dealing with obedience to the law of the supernatural Torah, laid so much emphasis on inwardly accepting, in the heart, the outer yoke of the commandments and the yoke of the Kingdom of Heaven. When the rabbis described the inner, imaginary state of Israel, they merely repeated the traits of the outer state of the nation: sovereignty based upon an act of supreme will, overcoming the facts of geography and politics alike.

Yet these imagined facts indeed corresponded to the realities of power, which tended to favor the local over the regional, let alone the imperial, authority. It was difficult to move troops about, except by marching them from place to place. It was therefore easy to build a large state, since little ones could not easily cooperate to defend themselves. But the superstates, once formed, found it difficult to control their components. This meant that the inner discipline exerted by people who believed in a law in common proved more effective in establishing a uniform policy than the formal discipline of contiguous territory or autochthonous government and army alike. So Israel the nation existed in the heart and soul of the Jewish people, with the consequence that the Land of Israel as an entity took on substance and meaning otherwise called into doubt or denied by the ordinary facts of life.

THE TALMUD IN ITS AGE

The Talmud contains virtually no reference to the most important events of the age in which it took shape and reached closure. We know about these events only from other sources. A document so reticent about events in its own day clearly wishes to be read as if composed in a vacuum. That claim, on the face of it, must be resisted. Merely because people pretend something has not happened, we cannot conclude that an otherwise well-attested event has not occurred. Insistence that nothing has changed never alters the facts of the matter. All that happens is that the pretense becomes one of the facts. We learn something about people who are unable to cope except through a massive effort to feign indifference. So, paradoxically, we observe a profound response indeed. On the basis of the evidence of the Talmud, ample though the book is, we could scarcely deduce the existence of the Roman Empire or of Christianity. Accordingly, we may hardly be guided by the insistence of the Talmud that it declare what does or does not demand attention. Part of the Talmud's powerful mode of coping with and shaping reality is that very insistence.

No one can claim that people made up the Talmud of the Land of Israel to deal with distant happenings, however crucial such happenings may have been. Nor shall we reduce the profoundly introspective discourse of the Talmud, preoccupied as it is with its own faraway issues, to a general message about the nature of the world and of Israel's place in it. At the same time, a simple reading of the ups-and-downs of the age (for Israel, mostly downs) surely is to be drawn into relationship with an equally unprepossessing account of the Talmud's own points of insistence: (1) Scriptural and textual certainty, (2) rabbis' authority, and (3) Israel's salvation.

Five events of fundamental importance for the history of Judaism occurred in the period in which the Talmud came to closure. All were well known in their own day: (1) the conversion of Constantine; (2) the fiasco of Julian's plan to rebuild the Temple in Jerusalem; (3) the depaganization of the Empire, accompanied by attacks on pagan temples and, along the way, synagogues; (4) the Christianization of the majority of the population of Palestine; and (5) the creation and closure of the Talmud of the Land of Israel. The Yerushalmi came into being in an age of high hope succeeded by disaster, a time of boundless expectations followed by bottomless despair — much like the age in which the Mishnah was composed. Admittedly, the Yerushalmi says nothing about Constantine or Julian, the proposed Temple, the devastation of synagogues, let alone mass apostasy (if, indeed, that occurred). But these things did happen. Everyone knew about them. Nothing that came in their wake can be perceived and interpreted wholly outside the realm of reality they define. Like famine, earthquake, plague, invasion — despair, disappointment, and disengagement with the old Israel are facts. They set the stage and the scene for all actors, whatever the dialogue. While defiance takes many forms, in my view the chief among these is the pretense of normality, serene reason in spite of all. In context we see that this was the Talmud's response: triumph over despair.

ISRAEL AMONG
THE NATIONS

The Jews of the Land of Israel looked out on the world through the eyes of a besieged garrison, seeing friends only rarely, and those motionless, on inaccessible, far-distant hilltops – or in Heaven. Israel's language, Aramaic, was not the language of the world to the north, northwest, and southwest. There people spoke Greek. Those who spoke Aramaic included many who were deemed by Rome, including Christian Rome, to be the other side. People on the margins worry not about civilization but about survival. Living in Aramaic rather than in Greek culture, with good connections to the enemy side of the contested eastern frontier, the Jews thus formed part of the third world, sandwiched between the Greek-speaking west of the Middle East, and the Iranian-speaking east. Along with other Semites, Armenians, and diverse linguistic and cultural groups, the Jews of the Land of Israel had no interest in guaranteeing the Roman civilization that had conquered them and destroyed their Temple. It is scarcely possible to point to a single document of the second, third, or fourth centuries in which a Jewish writer identifies with the civilization of Rome or regards the invasions from the east (let alone the north) as a world-historical threat. Siege was a calamity, not the end of civilization.

That is why Judaism bore within itself no theory of the world beyond its imaginary borders. Israel saw no need to provide the foundations of a world-philosophy and an international ethics that Judaism, for its part, viewed as null and degraded. So, in a word, Jews appear to have been both more insular than their neighbors and also more venturesome and less fearful of the strange peoples beyond the horizon. While the Greek-speaking citizen of the town feared the awful alien – not only invasion and siege, from which all suffered, but also a nameless chaos, a general collapse of worth and sense – the Jew, dissociated from the present order, did not. Christian apologists for Rome appealed to fears not felt by Israel. The upshot is that Judaism as represented by the Yerushalmi confronted the succession of one vision of empire by another, with little to say about the relative merits of either.

THE TRIUMPH
OF CHRISTIANITY

We come now to the paramount trait of the new world: the process of Christianization. The single most profound shift in the context of the Judaism of the West from ancient times onward to the nineteenth century, took place when the world in which Jews lived passed from pagan to Christian auspices and dominion. That shift took place in the very time and place in which the Yerushalmi came into being. When Judaism along with the rest of the world moved from the authority of the pagan Diocletian, persecutor of Christianity, to the rule of the Christian Constantine, everything familiar fell away. A new age stretching nearly into the twentieth century began. In many ways the new faith bore salient traits of the one out of which it had been born, Judaism, in its several forms of the day. What changed now for Judaism was not clear at the outset. Intent on constructing a reality insulated from the vagaries of history, the Talmud's great philosophers made little of the outer changes represented by the wars and dynastic struggles of the day. These happened far away. Judaism for its part had long enjoyed licit status, and had only to maintain its separation from the world at large to endure until the foreordained end of time. No one could foresee the progressive shift in the status of Judaism and with it, that of Israel, the Jewish people, as Christianity moved from persecuted to persecutor in little more than a generation.

The reason is that the conversion of Constantine brought no palpable changes in the circumstances in which Jews in their land lived out their lives. The world-historical meaning that Christians attached to that event speaks eloquently in all their writings. If Jews said nothing about it, that provides no indicator of what they were thinking. We cannot doubt, given the unchanging nature of Judaism's reflection on the meaning of events, that Jews, as much as Christians, tried to fit the event into some larger pattern or scheme of things. The special problem posed for Jews by the establishment of Christianity as a most-favored, then governing, religion, was the view that Christianity was a kind of heresy of Judaism, based on a wrong reading of the Torah. A move of the Empire from reverence for Zeus to adoration of Mithras meant nothing; paganism was what it was, lacking all differentiation.

Christianity was something else. It was different. It was like Judaism. If so, the trend of sages' speculation cannot have avoided the issue of the place in the messianic pattern of this remarkable turn. Since the Christians celebrated confirmation of the faith — Christ's messiahship — and, at the moment, Jews were hardly prepared to concur, it falls within known patterns for us to suppose that Constantine's conversion would have been identified with some dark moment prefiguring the dawn of the messianic age. That conclusion goes beyond idle speculation, though it cannot rise to the level of confirmed fact. If, however, the events of the day, about which Jews were amply informed and the point of which was joyfully, forcefully, and ubiquitously proclaimed by their Christian neighbors, failed to excite messianic speculation among Jews, then we deal with a unique moment in the entire history of Judaism. Worlds do not change orbit, but Israel watchfully scans the horizon for a new star. What showed up was a meteor.

THE MESSIANIC CRISIS

If people were watching for the dawn, the Emperor Julian's plan to rebuild the ruined Temple in Jerusalem must have dazzled their eyes. For while Constantine surely raised the messianic question, the Emperor Julian decisively answered it. In 361 the now-pagan Julian gave permission to rebuild the Temple. Work briefly got under way but stopped because of an earthquake. Julian died in battle soon afterward, and nothing came of the project. Yet the meaning of the plan was explicit. Julian wished to falsify the prophecy of Jesus that "not one stone of the Temple would be left upon another." We may take for granted that, since the prophecy had not been proven false, many concluded that it indeed had been shown true. We do not know that Jews in large numbers drew the conclusion that Jesus really was the Christ. But in the next half-century, Palestine gained a Christian majority. The Christians were not slow to claim that their faith had been vindicated. We need not speculate on the depth of despair felt by those Jews who had hoped the project would come to fruition, whether priests looking forward to a return to power through the reinstatement of the cult, or ordinary folk who took for granted that the rebuilding of the Temple would mark the coming of the Messiah.

The threat to Church and Christian state alike presented by the advent of a pagan emperor such as Julian made urgent the formation of a new and aggressive policy toward outsiders; caught in the net was Judaism, too. Jews were perceived as an enemy, though a negligible threat. They were to be protected, but degraded. But for paganism in its institutions and expressions, matters were otherwise. The Christian emperors who succeeded Julian, Theodosius II in particular, made certain that the Christian empire would never again face a mortal threat like that posed by Julian ("the Apostate"). This they did by rooting out the institutions and rites that had sustained the enemy within. First and foremost, the temples were closed and sacrifice prohibited. The sword unsheathed against the pagan cult-places was sharp but untutored. So it did not discriminate among non-Christian centers of divine service. Nor could those who wielded it, zealots of the faith in church and street, have been expected to make such fine distinctions. The Roman government protected synagogues and punished those who damaged them, in line with the policy of extirpating paganism while protecting a degraded Judaism. But the faithful of the Church had their own ideas. Accordingly, the assault against pagan temples spilled over into an ongoing program of attacking synagogue property.

At this time, moreover, a phenomenon without much precedent over the previous thousand years came into view: random attacks on Jews by reason of their faith, as distinct from organized struggles among contending forces, Jewish and other armies or mobs. The long-established Roman tradition of tolerating Judaism and Jews, extending from the time of Julius Caesar and applying both in law and in fact, now drew to a close. A new reality, at this time lacking all basis in custom and in the policy of state and Church alike, faced the Jews: physical insecurity in their own villages and towns. Jewish synagogues and homes housed the same thing, which was to be eradicated: "Judaism." A mark of exceptional Christian piety came to consist in violence against Jewish holy places, property, and persons. Coming in the aftermath of the triumph of Christianity, on the one side, and the decisive destruction of the Jews' hope for the rebuilding of the Temple, on the other, the hitherto unimagined war against the Jews, in the last third of the fourth century and the beginning of the fifth, raised once again those questions about the meaning of history that Constantine, at the beginning of the age at hand, had forced upon Israel's consciousness.

Jews had waited nearly three hundred years from the destruction of the Temple in 70 to the promise of Julian in 360-361. Julian had intended to falsify the prophecies that the Gospels had imputed to Jesus. This he stated explicitly. But, as we know, instead of being falsified, Jesus' prophecy had been validated. No stone had been left on another in the Temple, not after 70, not after 361, just as Jesus had predicted. Instead of a rebuilt Temple, the Jews looked out on a world in which even their synagogues came under threat, and along with them, their own homes and persons. What could prove more conclusively the truth of the Christians' claim than the worldly triumph of their Church? Resisted for so long, that claim called into question whether it was worth waiting any longer for a messiah who had not come. With followers proclaiming that the Messiah had come to possess the world, the question could hardly be avoided. The Land of Israel having become the Holy Land, the export of its sanctification in the form of the bones of saints and martyrs now began.

THE IMMEDIATE CONTEXT OF THE YERUSHALMI

In the result, the changes in the condition of Israel in its land were stunning. The shift was not so much political as religious. A second Israel had now come to the land, but with its own maps of the "Holy Land." The territory could never again be the same. No longer to be seen as mere pagans, who could be kept at arm's length, the new class, the Christians in the Holy Land, revered the same saints, serendipitously finding the body of Zechariah in 412 and that of Rabban Gamaliel and his sons in 415. Here was a situation without precedent, in an age lacking all preparation: a kind of Israel had come to power, claiming kinship to the same saints, access to the same Scriptures, service of the same, sole God, creator of the world and protector of Israel, revering the same place, and even participating in the same sacred history of Israel as Israel itself. If Israel's condition in its own land, now exposed to violence, and the state of Israel's synagogues everywhere, now subjected to everyday threats of destruction, were permitted to testify, then Israel's faith in the coming of the Messiah and in God's love and favor for its worship in the synagogues was apt to waver.

Before us is a familiar pattern: (1) messianic hope, (2) post-messianic disillusion, and (3) a holy book. This pattern had played itself out two hundred years earlier in the aftermath of the Bar Kokhba War (132-135). There had been a messianic war, a colossal defeat, then the formation of the Mishnah. This frame of mind was made articulate. We recall Justin's Trypho, an imaginary Jew who, about 150, had gone into exile after Bar Kokhba's war, and with whom Justin conducted an invented disputation. Trypho, the character invented by the Christian apologist, found in Christianity the correct interpretation for the pattern of events he had recently endured. Had he risen from the dead, that same imaginary Trypho would not have found perplexing the parallel events that occurred two centuries later. What happened now had already happened. What things had proved before, they proved again.

Christians were not slow to say so. Their program of settling upon the land a landscape of holy places, transforming through piety ordinary bones into relics and stones here and there into the locus of faith, changed the Land of Israel into the Holy Land. So the site of Judaism became the locative version of utopian, now universal Christianity. For two hundred years, matters would remain as they were, until Islam transformed the Mediterranean world, as successor faith for most of the Near and Middle East, North Africa, Spain, southern France, and Italy. When that happened, Israel would once more ask urgently about redemption.

THE ANTHOLOGY AT HAND

Now that we understand the context of the Yerushalmi, we may turn to the content. First, why do I give long abstracts? In seeing how the Talmud expresses its ideas, readers may draw conclusions from *how* things are said as much as from the assertions themselves.

Second, what do I hope to portray? I seek to grasp how the framers of a document drawn up in difficult days viewed humankind, and to describe through its details the theory of humanity and human potentiality that emerged among sages confronting an adverse and contentious setting. So I mean to present one group's theory of what counts and what truly matters in ourselves.

As we shall see, the sages at hand rely upon reason and criticism in the confrontation with the disorderly and difficult age at hand. So they believe the human mind can control or dispose of what happens. That is why the *way* they express their ideas, as much as *what* they wish to tell us, testifies to the main point.

But what, third, is the main point? The answer lies in the message that we can derive from the numerous specific messages the sages present. They speak of specific things; we seek the general and the whole. They never talk about abstract and large things such as disappointment and disintegration and decay. But the task they undertake determined that they should answer one set of questions rather than another. And the questions at hand dictated a focus upon uncertainty, defeat, disorder, and disillusion. So they went, seeking assurance, enduring defeat, overcoming disorder, substituting affirmation—perhaps illusion—for the betrayal, by events, of an old vision.

The sages of the Yerushalmi may claim one success. The group to whom they spoke, whose problems they took up, so listened to what they said as to overcome precisely the challenges before that generation—and succeeding ones, too. The result is that Israel, the old, disheartened, but enduring Israel after the flesh, did overcome and did endure. And the fundamental message of the hour spoke for age succeeding age. Long afterward, Israel's context provoked messages of lasting content. Not many sages of antiquity, or any other age, spoke so far beyond the grave and so long after their lifetime.

In what follows, I shall provide ample and accessible examples of how the Talmud's sages spoke and of what they wished to say about concrete issues of their day. Out of these sizable excerpts, I hope that a larger picture of humanity will emerge, or, at least, of an image of that sector of humanity to which sages spoke — namely, Israel, the Jewish people. All things attest to the particular, but each case may exemplify something general. If, through my selection and arrangement of sizable passages of the Yerushalmi, the Talmud of the Land of Israel, I am able to convey not only the image of humanity expressed in some small detail, through each passage, but also the image of humanity encompassed by them all, I shall have attained my modest goal. For I mean only to open a door long closed and to introduce a viewpoint and a world long left in isolation. In that way, I hope to add to our generation's yet modest treasure of examples of who we are and what we may become beyond calamity.

The simple logic of the ordering of topics requires little explanation. I begin, in the first five chapters, with the perennial themes of the Judaic religion: God, Israel, history, destiny, and salvation. In Chapters 6 through 10, I reconsider each of these themes in light of what is basic to the system and document at hand: the sage. We consider in particular and in general — matching the opening units — the sage in relationship to God and Israel and how he frames the issues of Torah, history, destiny, and salvation.

What I contribute is simple. First, I introduce each topic, chapter by chapter, explaining what I think is important. Second, I translate the passages and lay them out so that they may be readily understood in meaningful sequence. I include only brief annotations, where I think something is not immediately clear. So my picture emerges from what I have chosen and how I have arranged the selections. My message in the book as a whole is that the classic issues of Jewish existence undergo a complete revision and restatement in the encounter with the figure of the sage: the human being in God's image and likeness. In order to convey that message I first lay out these enduring issues, as they occur in the Yerushalmi. Then I conduct a reprise of these same issues, as they are restated in the encounter with the heroic person of the sage.

It remains to say the obvious. All the sages are men. No women play a significant part in the unfolding of the Yerushalmi's discussion and system. In this significant regard, ours is the first generation of Jews to aspire to include, in Jewish public discourse, that half of the Jewish people formerly treated as invisible. The fundamental conception of humanity in God's image –"male and female God created them"– need not, and should not, exclude women. But in the Yerushalmi, it does. Our age's task will reach fulfillment only when those who, in the age to come, will master and make use of the Yerushalmi, among all rabbinic writings, will transform its message. Only then will the Yerushalmi address the whole of the Jewish people with its call to sanctification, hence salvation. "Our sages" must now encompass women as much as men.

1
Death

To DISCOVER WHAT IS DISTINCTIVE in a system of belief and behavior, we had best start with what is not. In that way we may discern, in people's discussion of an experience common to us all, the distinctive viewpoints and social perspectives that set them apart.

No human experience is more universal than death, and no fact of life is more culture-bound than how we think about and approach dying. Death serves at once to unite us with, and to divide us from, one another. At issue here is how the sages of the Talmud of the Land of Israel frame the issue of dying and death, how they phrase their ideas, and what they choose to emphasize.

THE MORTALITY
OF HUMANITY

We begin with a citation from the Mishnah, given in boldface, followed by sages' commentary about what it means to be mortal and corrupt: who is humanity, and where we go. The second passage expresses the same spirit. We are dust and ashes. But the dust of which humanity (Adam) is made comes from the place where the altar of the holy Temple stood. So we come from the nexus between Heaven and earth, not only dirt but also the breath of life breathed into us by God. We are twin-things, dust of the altar, breath of God. And, at the end, we see how the soul leaves the body and goes its way.

Aqabiah ben Mehallalel says: Reflect upon three things, and you will not fall into the clutches of transgression: know from whence you came, whither you are going, and before whom you are going to have to give a full account of yourself. From whence do you come? From a putrid drop. Whither are you going? To a place of dust, worms, and maggots. And before whom are you going to have to give a full account of yourself? Before the King of kings of kings, the Holy One, blessed be He Mishnah Abot 3:1.

Rabbi Abba son of Rabbi Pappi, and Rabbi Joshua of Sikhnin in the name of Rabbi Levi: All three of them did Rabbi Aqabiah derive from a single verse of Scripture: Remember your Creator [BWR'K] Ecclesiastes 12:1. Remember your well [B'RK], your pit [BRK], your Creator [BWR'K]. *Your well* — the place from which you came. *Your pit* — the place to which you go. *Your Creator* — before whom you are going to give a full account of yourself. — YERUSHALMI SOTAH 2:2 V

Said Rabbi Judah ben Pazzi: The Holy One, blessed be He, took a spoonful of dirt from the place of the altar, and with it created the first man. He said: May he be created from the place of the altar and so endure. This is in line with that which is stated: Then the Lord God formed man of dust of the ground [and breathed into his nostrils the breath of life; and man became a living being] Genesis 2:7. And it is written: An altar of earth you shall make for Me [and sacrifice on it your burnt offerings and your peace offerings, your sheep and your cattle] Exodus 20:21. Just as "earth" stated later on refers to earth of the altar, so "earth" stated here refers to earth of the altar.

[My spirit shall not abide in man forever, for his is flesh,] but his days shall be a hundred and twenty years Genesis 6:3. The first man lived nearly a thousand years, and you say, but his days shall be a hundred and twenty years? But in one hundred and twenty years he returns [in the grave] to form as much dirt as fills a single spoonful of mould. —YERUSHALMI NAZIR 7:2 IV

They give testimony about the identity of a corpse only during a period of three days after death Mishnah Yebamot 16:3.

Rabbi Bereh and Rabbi Pappi, Rabbi Joshua of Sikhnin in the name of Rabbi Levi: For the first three days after death the soul floats above the body, thinking that it will return to the body. When the soul sees the body, that the appearance of the face has changed, it leaves the body and goes its way. And when three days have passed, the stomach swells up over the face and says to it, Here is what you have stolen and seized by violence.

Rabbi Haggai in the name of Rabbi Josiah proves the case from this verse of Scripture: Behold, I spread dung upon your faces and even the dung of your offerings Malachi 2:3. At that moment: He feels only the pain of his own body, and he mourns only for himself Job 14:22. —YERUSHALMI YEBAMOT 16:3 IV

DEATH'S INTRUSION: UNTIMELY, UNWANTED WHENEVER IT COMES

Death not only ends life, it also contradicts life's logic. So whenever we die, it is not wanted and not timely. How to cope with that illogic? The passage below insists that, whenever we die, it is the right time, the time of God's choice.

When Rabbi Hiyya bar Adda, the nephew of bar Qappara died, Resh Laqish [accepted condolences] on his account because he [Resh Laqish] had been his teacher. We may say that a person's student is as beloved to him as his son.

And he expounded concerning [Rabbi Hiyya] this verse: My beloved has gone down to his garden, to the beds of spices, to pasture his flock in the gardens, and to gather lilies Song of Songs 6:2. It is not necessary [to say to the beds of spices]. [It is redundant if you interpret the verse literally, for most gardens have spice beds.] Rather [interpret the verse as follows]: My beloved—this is God; has gone down to his garden—this is the world; to the beds of spices—this is Israel; to pasture his flock in the gardens—these are the nations of the world; and to gather lilies—these are the righteous whom he takes from their midst.

This may be explained with a parable. A king had a son who was very beloved to him. What did the king do? He planted an orchard for him. As long as the son acted according to his father's will, he used to search throughout the world to seek the beautiful saplings of the world to plant them in his orchard. And when his son angered him he went and cut down all his saplings. So long as Israel acts according to God's will, He searches throughout the world to seek the righteous persons of the nations of the world and bring them and join them to Israel, as He did with Jethro and Rahab. And when they anger Him, He removes the righteous from their midst.

Rabbi Hiyya bar Abba and his associates, and some say it was Rabbi Yose ben Halafta and his associates, and some say it was Rabbi Aqiba and his associates, were sitting discussing Torah under a certain fig tree. And each day the owner of the fig tree would awaken early and gather [the ripe figs]. They said: Perhaps he suspects [that we are taking his figs]. Let us change our place. The next day the owner of the fig tree came and said to them: My masters, you have deprived me of the one commandment you were accustomed to fulfill with me [under my tree]. They said to him: We feared perhaps you suspected us [of taking your figs]. The next morning he let them see [why he picked the figs early]. He waited until the sun shone upon them and his figs became worm-eaten. At that time they said: The owner of the fig tree knows when it is the right time to pick a fig and he picks it. So, too, God knows when it is the right time to take the righteous from the world and he takes them.

When Rabbi Bun bar Rabbi Hiyya died, Rabbi Zeira came up and in regard to him he expounded this verse: **Sweet is the sleep of a laborer whether he eats little or much; but the surfeit of the rich will not let him sleep** Ecclesiastes 5:11. It does not say whether he sleeps but rather whether he eats little or much. To whom may Rabbi Bun bar Rabbi Hiyya be compared? To a king who hired many workers, and one of those workers excelled very much in his work. What did the king do? He took him and walked with him through the long and short rows of crops. Towards evening when the workers came to be paid, he gave him a full day's wages with them. The workers complained and said: We toiled all day and this one toiled only two hours, and he gave him a full day's wages! The king said to them: This one worked more in two hours [and accomplished more] than you did in a whole day. So Rabbi Bun toiled in the Torah for twenty-eight years [and learned] more than an aged student could learn in a hundred years.

When Rabbi Simeon bar Zebid died, Rabbi Ilya came up and in regard to him expounded as follows: Four things are essential for the world. But if they are lost they can be replaced [as we see in the following verse]: Surely there is a mine for silver, and a place for gold which they refine. Iron is taken out of the earth, and copper is smelted from the ore. Job 28:1-2. If these are lost they can be replaced. But if a disciple of the sages died, who shall bring us his replacement? Who shall bring us his exchange? But where shall wisdom be found and where is the place of understanding? Job 28:12. It is hid from the eyes of all living Job 28:21. —YERUSHALMI BERAKHOT 2:7 II [Translated by Tzvee Zahavy]

The righteous always die when they "should." God knows the right time. But what of the ones who should have long life and die young, and the bereaved parents of children who pass on before their day? The next abstract solves that problem to the satisfaction of those who see it as a problem. Once people assume there must be a certain justice, a right logic, to death, they also imagine that, one way or the other, there is.

Nehuniah digs ditches for water Mishnah Sheqalim 5:1: For he was a digger of ditches and caves [for water], and he knew under which stone was a spring of water, and under which stone was dry heat, and how far its dry heat reaches.

Said Rabbi Eliezer: Yet his son died of thirst.

Said Rabbi Hanina: He who said: The All-Merciful is forgiving—may his bowels bulge out. But [God] is long-suffering but ultimately collects what is coming to Him.

Said Rabbi Aha: It is written: Our God comes, He does not keep silence, before Him is a devouring fire, round about Him a mighty tempest Psalms 50:3. He is meticulous with them as with a thread like a hair.

Said Rabbi Yose: It is not on the basis of that verse of Scripture, but rather on the basis of the following: He is fearful for all those that are round about Him Psalms 89:8. Fear of Him is greater for those that are near than for those that are far.

Rabbi Haggai in the name of Rabbi Samuel bar Nahum: There is the story of a pious man, who was a digger of wells, ditches, and cisterns [to provide water] for those who would pass by [for use on their journey]. One time his daughter was en route to be married, and a river swept her away. Everybody came up to him and wanted to give him comfort, and he would not accept consolation. Rabbi Phineas ben Yair came to him and wanted to comfort him, but he would not accept consolation. He said [to those round about]: Is this your pious man?! They said to [Rabbi Phineas]: Rabbi, this is what this man does, and this is what happened to him! He said to them: It is not possible that he should honor his Creator by good deeds involving water, and [God] should smite him with water. Forthwith the word came to the town, The daughter of that man is coming. Some say that she showed herself on a cloud, and there are those who say that an angel came down in the guise of Rabbi Phineas ben Yair and saved her. —YERUSHALMI SHEQALIM 5:1 VIII

WHEN SAGES DIE

Moving from the general to the particular, we come to the center of the Yerushalmi's construct of humanity, the sage himself. The death of a sage defines an event in the supernatural, as much as in the natural, world. Accordingly, supernature responds through natural events. When sages die, they accept their fate—the gift of mortality—thinking only of the cultic uncleanness to come with their own corpse, when they breathe their last. Why so? None fears death. Faith in God, taking refuge in God—these define the way beyond the end. Facing death, none asks why he has been forsaken, and all affirm salvation. Theirs is a vision of a world at home in God's providence. Just as people die when they should, not before but when God chooses, so sages die at just the right moment. None complains, none mourns himself. Death is a celebration. For the pious person, death is a privilege, a reunion.

When Rabbi Aha died, a star appeared at noon.

When Rabbi Hanan died, the statues bowed low.

When Rabbi Yohanan died, the statues bowed down. They said that [this was to indicate] there were no icons like him [so beautiful as Yohanan himself].

When Rabbi Hanina of Bet Hauran died, the Sea of Tiberias split open. They said that [this was to commemorate the miracle that took place] when he went up to intercalate the year, and the sea split open before him.

When Rabbi Hoshaia died, the palm of Tiberias fell down.

When Rabbi Isaac ben Eliasheb died, seventy [infirm] thresholds of houses in Galilee were shaken down. They said that [this was to commemorate the fact that] they [were shaky and] had depended on his merit [for the miracle that permitted them to continue to stand].

When Rabbi Samuel bar Rabbi Isaac died, cedars of the land of Israel were uprooted. They said that [this was to take note of the fact that] he would take a branch [of a cedar] and [dance, so] praising a bride [at her wedding, and thereby giving happiness to the bride]. The rabbis would ridicule him [for lowering himself by doing so]. Rabbi Zeira said to them: Leave him be. Does the old man not know what he is doing? When [Rabbi Samuel] died, a flame came forth from Heaven and intervened between his bier and the congregation. For three hours there were voices and thunderings in the world: Come and see what a sprig of cedar has done for this old man! [Further,] an echo came forth and said: Woe that Samuel bar Rabbi Isaac has died, the doer of merciful deeds.

When Rabbi Yose bar Halafta died, the gutters ran with blood in Laodicea. They said [that the reason was] that he had given his life for the rite of circumcision.

When Rabbi Abbahu died, the pillars of Caesarea wept. The [gentiles] said [that the reason was] that [the pillars] were celebrating. The Israelites said to them: And do those who are distant [such as yourselves] know why those who are near [we ourselves] are raising a cry?

When Rabbi Abbahu lay dying, they brought before him thirteen lamps kindled with balsam wood. He said to them: For whom are all these? They said to him: They are for you. He said to them:

And are all these for Abbahu? I have labored in vain, I have spent my strength for nothing and vanity; yet surely my right is with the Lord, and my recompense with my God Isaiah 49:4. The Holy One, blessed be He, shows the righteous in this world the reward that is coming to them, so that when their soul is satisfied, they may go into their sleep. It may be compared to a king who made a banquet, and on a cloth he made a design of all the foods to be served at the banquet. When the guests entered, they saw [the cloth] and their souls were sated, so they went into a deep sleep.

Zabedai bar Levai and Rabbi Yose bar Piteres and Rabbi Joshua ben Levi respectively cited [one of the following] three verses when they were dying: One of them said: Therefore let every one who is godly offer prayer to Thee Psalms 32:6. And one of them said: But let all who take refuge in Thee rejoice, let them ever sing for joy Psalms 5:12. And one of them said: O how abundant is Thy goodness, which Thou has laid up for those who fear Thee and wrought for those who take refuge in Thee Psalms 31:20. — YERUSHALMI ABODAH ZARAH 3:1 II

Rabbi Jacob bar Idi in the name of Rabbi Joshua ben Levi: When Rabban Yohanan ben Zakkai lay dying, he commanded, saying: Clear the courtyard [of articles susceptible to uncleanness] because of uncleanness [consequent upon my death—since the corpse produces contamination], and prepare a throne for Hezekiah, king of Judah.

Rabbi Eliezer, his disciple, when he lay dying, gave orders, saying: Clear out the courtyard because of uncleanness, and prepare a throne for Rabban Yohanan ben Zakkai. And there are those who say: The one whom his master envisioned is the one whom he envisioned.

The patriarchate wanted to marry into the house of Pazzi, and he did not agree. He told them that they should not be ashamed. When he lay dying, he gave orders and said: Clear out the courtyard because of uncleanness, and prepare a throne for Jehoshaphat, king of Judah. They said: Let this one, who pursued honor, come after that one, who fled from honor. —YERUSHALMI SOTAH 9:16 II

2

Israel's Condition

THE HUMAN CONDITION, stark and unadorned, begins in breath and ends in dust. Israel's existence forms a metaphor of humanity, misery caught in a gossamer web, in a myth of glory. Just as humanity, in God's image, ends in the grave, so Israel, God's first love, lives out its life in the thrall of the gentiles. Just as humanity would overcome the grave through resurrection, Israel too hopes to throw off the paradox of its condition by being saved from the nations and for the service of God. Accordingly, Israel's fate shapes the paradigm of humanity's existence, and Israel's salvation presents a metaphor of humanity's hope.

THE TEMPLE THAT WAS DESTROYED

The event that defined the world for Israel took place in 70 C.E., the destruction of the Temple of Jerusalem. Viewed objectively, that event freed Judaism from the burden of animal sacrifice — progressively disdained among the pagan intellectuals of the age.

The inner life of the Jewish people found release from focus exclusively on a single locale, so that Jews living throughout the world found it possible without apology or concession of secondary status to worship God through prayer and study and a holy way of life. No longer did those living long distances from Jerusalem have to measure their worth in relationship to that distant holy place. Had the Temple and its bloody cult continued, it would surely have fallen into desuetude, whether or not Jews maintained control of Jerusalem. By the dramatic way in which it reached its final moment, the Temple provided a perpetually powerful image of loss and focus for hope for restoration and rebirth for Israel at large.

The greatest service that the Temple rendered for the people who had sustained it for so long lay in its suffering ultimate destruction. Not once but many times, from 586 B.C.E. onward in fact, the Temple had been taken and destroyed, by both gentiles and Jews. Each such occasion then marked a moment, an epoch in Israel's ongoing relationship with God: destruction because of sin, restoration through repentance and reconciliation.

You find that when Nebuchadnezzar came up here, he came and enthroned himself at Dephne, near Antioch. The Great Sanhedrin came forth to greet him, saying to him: The time for destroying this House [the Temple] has come.

He said to them: The one whom I made king over you — give him to me, and I shall go along my way.

They came and told Jehoiachin, king of Judea: Nebuchadnezzar wants you.

When he heard that from them, he took the keys of the Temple, went up to the roof of the Temple, and said before Him: Lord of the world! In the past we were faithful to You, and the keys to Your house were handed over to us. Now that we are no longer faithful to You, lo, here are Your keys, given back to You.

Two Amoras: One said: He threw them upward, and they did not come down again. The other said: A kind of hand came forth and took them from his hand.

When all the nobles of Judea saw this, they went up to the roofs of their houses and threw themselves down and died. That is in line with what is written, The oracle concerning the valley of vision. What do you mean that you have gone up, all of you, to the housetops, you who are full of shoutings, tumultuous city, exultant town? Your slain are not slain with the sword or dead in battle Isaiah 22:1-2. —YERUSHALMI SHEQALIM 6:2 III

From the perspective of the third and fourth centuries, the ruined Temple supplied the governing metaphor for the condition of Israel and of God in the world. Its restoration then would signal Israel's reconciliation with God and God's renewal on earth. That is the message delivered in a subtle way by the account of the destruction of the first Temple of Jerusalem in 586 B.C.E. The cessation of the offerings, after long years in which God had miraculously secured the perpetual daily whole offering, signified the end.

Rabbi Simon in the name of Rabbi Joshua ben Levi: In the days of the Greek Empire [when Jerusalem was besieged], they would let down two baskets containing gold, and they would send up two rams [for the daily whole offering]. One time they let down to them two baskets of gold, and they sent up to them two lambs. At that moment the Holy One, blessed be He, opened their eyes, and they found two lambs in the chamber of the lambs. It was in regard to that moment that Rabbi Judah ben Abba gave testimony concerning the daily whole offering brought in the morning, that it was offered at the fourth hour [Mishnah Eduyyot 6:1].

Said Rabbi Levi: Also in the time of this evil kingdom [that is, in the time of the Roman siege in 70 C.E.], they would let down to them two baskets of gold, and they would send up to them two lambs. Finally they let down to them two baskets of gold, and they sent up to them two pigs. The basket had not gotten halfway up the wall, before the pig[s] pressed [their] nails against the wall and lept forty *parasangs* out of the Land of Israel. At that moment the sins [of Israel] brought it about that the daily whole offering was cancelled, and the House [the Temple] was laid waste. —YERUSHALMI TAANIT 4:5 II

The following excerpt then vividly presents (in the Tosefta's version) a picture of both the loss and the restoration.

It has been taught: Rabbi Yose says: They assign a meritorious matter to a day that merits it, and a disadvantageous matter to a bad day.

When the Temple was destroyed the first time [in 586 B.C.E.], it was the day after the Sabbath and the year after the Sabbatical year. And it was the watch of Jehoiarib, and it was the ninth of Ab.

And so in the case of the destruction of the Second Temple [in 70 C.E.]. And the Levites were standing on their platform and singing, And He has brought upon them their own iniquity, and He will cut them off in their own evil Psalms 94:23.

[Tosefta Taanit 3:9 adds:] Now tomorrow, when the Temple-house will be rebuilt, what will they sing? Blessed be the Lord, the God of Israel, from everlasting to everlasting 1 Chronicles 16:36. [Blessed be the Lord, the God of Israel] who alone does wondrous things. Blessed be His glorious name [forever; may His glory fill the whole earth. Amen and Amen] Psalms 72:18-19. —YERUSHALMI TAANIT 4:5 IX

THE MESSIAH WHO FAILED

The principal message of the Yerushalmi concerning Israel's redemption was to rely upon God, to wait patiently and submissively for God's intervention and to make the people worthy of it. The condition of the people of Israel surely accorded with such a message. They were not numerous and not popular, not in command of large tracts of land and not united in any one place. They had fought their wars and lost them. Imagining that the defeat came because of their own fault gave them that necessary conviction that they controlled their fate, when, in fact, others did. Accordingly, the message of the sages served to help Israel accommodate its fantastic understanding of itself and its own importance to the context in which it had to live out its national life. Israel remained God's first love, first fruit of God's harvest. The victorious pagans were null, except as they served God's purposes. Israel controlled what happened. The governing facts lay within the heart and soul of the people, essentially all they could in fact determine.

The message passively to submit to the nations, but actively to accept God's dominion, took shape in sages' tales about the messiah who claimed to do just the opposite, and whose catastrophic defeat had thrown Israel into its present, continuing, and chronic condition of dismay and crisis. Bar Kokhba (the warrior-messiah who led the disastrous rebellion against Rome from 132 to 135 C.E.) had rejected God's rule and help and presumed to do things on his own and at a time of his choosing. Regard the result.

The various defeats flow together, much as a single discourse will mention several times at which the Temple was destroyed. In the passage below we deal with what appears to be a reference to the Roman emperor Trajan, who put down a rebellion of the Jews of the Diaspora in 116 C.E., and in the second selection, with stories mainly about Bar Kokhba.

In the time of Tronianus, the evil one, a son was born to him on the ninth of Ab, and [the Israelites] were fasting. His daughter died on Hanukkah, and [the Israelites] lit candles. His wife sent a message to him: Instead of going out to conquer the barbarians, come and conquer the Jews, who have rebelled against you.

He thought the trip would take ten days, but he arrived in five. He came and found the Israelites occupied in the study of the Torah, with the following verse: The Lord will bring a nation against you from afar, from the end of the earth, as swift as the eagle flies, a nation whose language you do not understand Deuteronomy 28:49.

He said to them: With what are you occupied?

They said to him: With thus-and-so.

He said to them: [I] thought that it would take ten days to make the trip, and I arrived in five days [proving God is on my side].

His legions surrounded the [Jewish soldiers] and killed them. He said to the women: Submit to my legions, and I shall not kill you.

They said to him: What you did to the ones who have fallen, do also to us who are yet standing.

He mingled their blood with the blood of their men, until the blood flowed into the ocean as far as Cyprus. At that moment the horn of Israel was cut off, and it is not destined to return to its place until the son of David will come. —YERUSHALMI SUKKAH 5:1 VII

As we see, the discourse flows on and on, reaching in all directions and covering a considerable span of Israel's history, backward in time to the first destruction, forward to the Messiah's coming. No one imagines that Bar Kokhba had been a messiah, let alone the Messiah.

Betar [the last stronghold of Bar Kokhba] was taken Mishnah Taanit 4:5: Rabbi would derive by exegesis twenty-four tragic events from the verse: The Lord has destroyed without mercy all the habitations of Jacob; in His wrath He has broken down the strongholds of the daughter of Judah; He has brought down to the ground in dishonor the kingdom and its rulers Lamentations 2:2.

Rabbi Yohanan derived sixty from the same verse.

Did Rabbi Yohanan then find more than did Rabbi in the same verse?

[No,] but because Rabbi lived nearer to the destruction of the Temple, there were in the audience old men who remembered what had happened, and when he gave his exegesis, they would weep and fall silent and get up and leave.

It has been taught: Said Rabbi Judah ben Rabbi Ilai: Barukh, my master, would interpret as follows: So Jacob went near to Isaac his father, who felt him and said: The voice is the voice of Jacob, but the hands are the hands of Esau Genesis 27:22. The voice of Jacob [=Israel] cries out on account of what the hands of Esau [=Rome] did to him at Betar.

Rabbi Simeon ben Yohai taught: Aqiba, my master, would interpret the following verse: A star [KOKHAB] shall come forth out of Jacob—A disappointment [KOZEBA] shall come forth out of Jacob.

Rabbi Aqiba: When he saw Bar Kozeba, he said: This is the King Messiah. Said to him Rabbi Yohanan ben Toreta: Aqiba! Grass will grow on your cheeks, and the Messiah will not yet have come!

Said Rabbi Yohanan: Upon orders ["voice"] of Caesar Hadrian in Betar, they killed eight hundred thousand. Said Rabbi Yohanan: There were eighty thousand pairs of trumpeters that surrounded Betar. Each one was in charge of a number of troops.

Ben Kozeba was there, and he had two hundred thousand troops who, as a sign of loyalty, had cut off their little finger. Sages sent word to him: How long are you going to turn Israel into a maimed people? He said to them: How otherwise is it possible to test them? They replied to him: Whoever cannot uproot a cedar of Lebanon while riding on his horse will not be inscribed on your military rolls.

So there were two hundred thousand who qualified in one way and another two hundred thousand who qualified in another way.

When [Bar Kokhba] would go forth to battle, he would say: Lord of the world! Do not help and do not hinder us! Hast Thou not rejected us, O God? Thou dost not go forth, O God, with our armies Psalms 60:12.

Three-and-a-half years did Hadrian besiege Betar. Rabbi Eleazar of Modiin would sit on sackcloth and ashes and pray every day, saying: Lord of the ages! Do not judge in accord with strict judgment this day! Do not judge in accord with strict judgment this day!

Hadrian wanted to go to him. A Samaritan said to [Hadrian]: Do not go to him, until I see what he is doing, and so hand over the city [of Betar] to you [Make peace ... for you.]

He got into the city through a drainpipe. He went and found Rabbi Eleazar of Modiin standing and praying. He pretended to whisper something into his ear.

The townspeople saw him do this and brought him to Bar Kozeba. They told him: We saw this man having dealings with your friend.

He said to [the Samaritan]: What did you say to him, and what did he say to you?

He said to him: If I tell you, then [Hadrian] will kill me, and if I do not tell you, then you will kill me. It is better that the king kill me, and not you. He said to me: I shall hand over my city [I shall make peace ...].

[Bar Kokhba] turned to Rabbi Eleazar of Modiin. He said to him: What did this Samaritan say to you? He replied: Nothing. He said to him: What did you say to him? He said to him: Nothing.

[Bar Kokhba] gave [Eleazar] one good kick and killed him.
Forthwith an echo came forth and proclaimed the following verse:
Woe to my worthless shepherd, who deserts the flock! May the
sword smite his arm and his right eye! Let his arm be wholly
withered, his right eye utterly blinded! Zechariah 11:17. You have mur-
dered Eleazar of Modiin, the right arm of all Israel, and their right
eye. Therefore may the right arm of that man [Bar Kokhba]
whither, may his right eye be utterly blinded!

Forthwith Betar was taken, and Ben Kozeba was killed.

They brought his head and displayed it to Hadrian. He said:
Who killed this man? The Samaritan said: I killed him. He said
to him: Show me his corpse. He showed him his corpse. He found
a large snake wrapped around him. He said: If it were not God who
had killed him, who could have killed him? And concerning him
he cited the following verse: How should one chase a thousand,
and two put ten thousand to flight, unless their Rock had sold
them, and the Lord had given them up? Deuteronomy 32:30.

Now they kept slaughtering [the Jews] until a horse sank into
blood up to his nose, and the blood would pick up heavy stones,
weighing forty *seahs* until the blood flowed four *mils* into the sea.
(Now, if you want to suppose that Betar was near the sea, in fact
it was forty *mils* from the sea.)

They say: They found three hundred babies' skulls on a single
rock, and they found three baskets of boxes for *tefillin*, each weighing nine *seahs*. And there are those who say: They found nine, each
weighing three *seahs*.

It has been taught: Rabban Simeon ben Gamaliel says: There
were five hundred schoolhouses in Betar. The smallest of them had
no fewer than five hundred children. They said: If the enemy
comes against us, with these quills we shall go forth against them
and put their eyes out. On account of the sins that caused the
tragedy, [the Romans] wrapped each one of the children in his
scroll and burned him, and out of them all, I alone have survived.
He cited in his own regard the following verse of Scripture: My
eyes cause me grief at the fate of all the maidens of my city Lamentations 3:51.

The evil Hadrian had a large vineyard, eighteen *mil* by eighteen *mil*. It was of the dimension of the distance from Tiberias to

Sepphoris. They surrounded it by a wall made of the bones of those who were slain in Betar, as tall as the height of a man, and as broad as the extent of the breadth of the hands. And [Hadrian] did not decree that the bones might be buried until another king came along and decreed that they might be buried.

Said Rabbi Huna: When those who were slain in Betar were given for burial, the blessing . . . "who is good and who does good . . ." was framed [in the prayer]. "Who is good . . ." for the bodies did not rot. "Who does good . . ." for the bodies were handed over for burial.

There were two brothers in a destroyed village. The Romans attacked [the village] and killed the people. They said: To end the matter, let us bring a crown for their heads. They said: Let us try one more time. They went forth [to attack the Romans again]. An old man met them and said to them: May your Creator be your help!

[One of the brothers] said to him: May He not help nor support us: Has Thou not rejected us, O God! Thou dost not go forth, O God, with our armies Psalms 60:12.

There were two cedars on the Mount of Olives. Under one of them there were four stalls, selling food preserved in a condition of cultic cleanness [to be eaten in Jerusalem]. And from one they would produce forty *seahs* weight of pigeons a month, and from these they would provide bird-offerings for all Israel.

From Simeon's Gate they would put forth three hundred barrels of thin cakes among the poor every Sabbath eve. Then why was it destroyed? There is one who says: It was because of fornication. There is one who says: It was because they would play ball [waste their time, instead of studying Torah].

There were ten thousand villages in the Royal Mountains. Rabbi Eleazar ben Harsom owned a thousand of them and, for them, a thousand ships in the sea. And all of them were destroyed. For three of the villages [alone] the census covering them had to be brought up to Jerusalem in a wagon. These were Kabul, Shihin, and Migdol Sebayya. All three of them were destroyed: Kabul, because of contention; Shihin, because of witchcraft; Migdol Sebayya, because of fornication.

There were three villages, each one of them twice as populous as those who went forth from Egypt: Kefar Bish, Kefar Shihelayya, and Kefar Dikhraya. Why was it called Kefar Bish ["evil"]? Because they did not welcome wayfarers. Why was it called Kefar Shihelayya ["cress"]? Because they reared their children as carefully as cress is cultivated. And why did they call it Kefar Dikhraya ["male"]? Because the women produced only male children.

Said Rabbi Yohanan: Eighty pairs of brothers, who were priests, married eighty pairs of sisters, who were daughters of priests, on a single night in the town of Gopna, exclusive of brothers who were without sisters, sisters who were without brothers, exclusive of Levites, exclusive of Israelites. Said Rabbi Yohanan: There were eighty stalls of those who weave material for traveling cloaks in Migdal Sebayya ["Weavers' Tower"]. Said Rabbi Hiyya bar Ba: There were eighty stores selling food preserved in the condition of cultic cleanness in Kefar Imra ["Lamb-town"]. Rabbi Jeremiah in the name of Rabbi Hiyya bar Ba: There were eighty metal chests in Shihin. Said Rabbi Yannia: There is no such a chest [as this] in our time.

Rabbi Zeira in the name of Rabbi Huna says: That was the least of the priestly watches, and it would bring forth eighty-five thousand apprentice-priests. Said Rabbi Yohanan: Eighty thousand apprentice-priests were killed because of the shedding of the blood of Zechariah.

Rabbi Yudan asked Rabbi Aha: Where did they kill Zechariah, in the Women's Court [of the Temple] or in the Israelites' Court? He said to him: It was neither in the Women's Court nor in the Israelites' Court, but in the courtyard reserved for the priests. And they did not treat his blood either as one does with the blood of a ram or as one does with the blood of a deer. There it is written: Any man also of the people of Israel, or of the strangers that sojourn among them, who takes in hunting any beast or bird that may be eaten shall pour out its blood and cover it with dust Leviticus 17:13. And here it is written: For the blood she has shed is still in the midst of her; she put it on the bare rock, she did not pour it upon the ground to cover it with dust Ezekiel 24:7. And why? To rouse My wrath, to take vengeance, I have set on the bare rock the blood she has shed, that it may not be covered Ezekiel 24:8.

Seven sins did the Israelites commit on that day. They killed priest, prophet, and judge. They spilled innocent blood. They contaminated the courtyard. And it was a Sabbath that coincided with the Day of Atonement as well.

Now when Nebuzaradan came here, he saw the blood bubbling up. He said to them: What is this? They said to him: It is the blood of the bullocks, sheep, and rams that we offer on the altar. Forthwith he brought bullocks, sheep, and rams, and slaughtered them on it, and still the blood was bubbling up. Since they did not confess to him, he ordered them suspended on the gallows for torture. They said: It appears that the Holy One, blessed be He, wants to exact from our hand vengeance for his blood.

They said to him: It is the blood of a priest, prophet, and judge, who prophesied against us concerning everything that you are now doing to us, and we rose up against him and killed him. Forthwith he brought eighty thousand apprentice-priests and slaughtered them, and still the blood bubbled up. At that moment he grew angry [at the blood], and said to it: What do you want? Should we destroy your entire nation on your account?

Forthwith the Holy One, blessed be He, was filled with mercy, and He said: Now if this one, who is a mere mortal and cruel, is filled with mercy for my children, I concerning whom it is written: For the Lord your God is a merciful God; He will not fail you or destroy you or forget the covenant with your fathers which He swore to them Deuteronomy 4:31, how much the more so [should I have mercy on them]! Forthwith he gave a sign to the blood, and it was swallowed up where it was.

Said Rabbi Yohanan: Eighty thousand apprentice-priests fled to the stoves of the Temple, and they were burned up. And of all of them there survived only Joshua ben Yehosedeq, the high priest. This is in line with that which is said: And the Lord said to Satan, The Lord rebuke you, O Satan! The Lord who has chosen Jerusalem rebuke you! Is this not a brand plucked from the fire? Zechariah 3:2.

Said Rabbi Yohanan: Eighty thousand apprentice-priests were [taken by] the army of Nebuchadnezzar, and they [fled] to the Ishmaelites. They said to them: Give us something to drink, because we are thirsty. They brought them salty things and skins that were blown up with air. They said to them: Eat and drink. When one of them opened a skin and put it on his mouth, the air that was in it burst forth and choked him. That is in line with what is written: The oracle concerning Arabia. In the thickets in Arabia you will lodge, O caravans of Dedanites. To the thirsty bring water, meet the fugitive with bread, O inhabitants of the land of Tema Isaiah 21:13-14. Those who were located in the "forest of Lebanon" [=the Temple, built of the cedars of Lebanon] now are in "the thickets of Arabia." "Caravans of Dedanites"–the Ishmaelites follow in the ways of the Dedanites, for as to him who was thirsty, it was not the case that, "To the thirsty they bring water."

Then God opened her eyes, and she saw a well of water; and she went, and filled the skin with water, and gave the lad a drink Genesis 21:19. It was not to win your thanks that they came to you. They were wandering in the wilderness because of the sword that was unsheathed, since they did not want to keep the years of release. That is in line with the verse which follows: But the seventh year you shall let it rest and lie fallow, that the poor of your people may eat; and what they leave the wild beasts may eat. You shall do likewise with your vineyard, and with your olive grove Exodus 23:11.

It was because the bow was drawn taut, for they did not want to observe the Sabbaths. That is in line with what is written: In those days I saw in Judah men treading wine presses on the Sabbath, and bringing in heaps of grain and loading them on asses; and also wine, grapes, figs, and all kinds of burdens, which they brought into Jerusalem on the Sabbath day; and I warned them on the day when they sold food Nehemiah 13:15.

It was because of the weight of the war, for they had not wanted to engage in the struggles of the Torah. That is in line with what is written: Wherefore it is said in the Book of the Wars of the Lord, "Waheb in Suphah, and the valleys of the Amon" Numbers 21:14.

Said Rabbi Yohanan: Between Gabbath and Antipatris there were sixty myriads of townships. The smallest among them was Beth Shemesh. Now what is written concerning that town? And He slew some of the men of Beth Shemesh, because they looked into the ark of the Lord; He slew seventy men of them, and the people mourned because the Lord had made a great slaughter among the people 1 Samuel 6:19.

And these were in only one direction. And now if you tried to stick sixty myriads of reeds there, it would not hold them. Said Rabbi Hanina: [The reason is that] the Land of Israel has shrunk.

Said Rabbi Zeira: Come and take note of how the Land of Israel is impudent, that it continues to produce crops [even though so much of the Land has been destroyed through fire and brimstone]. How does the Land produce as it does? Two Amoras: One said: It is because [the dead] fertilize it. The other said: It is because [the dead] turn over the dirt. There was the case of someone who was planting seed in the valley of Arbela. He pushed in his hand and drew out burning soil, which had burned up the seed.

It was taught: Rabbi Yose says: For fifty-two years no bird appeared in flight in the Land of Israel. What is the scriptural prooftext for this view? **Both the birds of the air and the beasts have fled and are gone** Jeremiah 9:10.

Said Rabbi Hanina: Forty years before the Israelites went into exile to Babylonia, they planted date-palms in Babylonia, since they wanted to have something sweet, for that prepares the tongue to study Torah.

Said Rabbi Hanina, son of Rabbi Abbahu: Seven hundred species of clean fish, eight hundred species of clean locusts, and fowl without number, all went into exile with the Israelites to Babylonia. And when they came back, all of them came back with them, except for the fish called "Shibuta." And how in the world did fish go into exile? Rabbi Huna bar Joseph said: They went into exile through the great deep [in the waters under the earth], and through the great deep they returned.

Said Rabbi Yohanan: Fortunate is he who sees the fall of Palmyra, for she was a partner in the destruction of the First Temple and in the destruction of the Second Temple. In the destruction of the First Temple she provided eighty thousand bowmen. In the destruction of the Second Temple she provided eighty thousand bowmen.

The city was ploughed up Mishnah Taanit 4:5:

Rufus—may his bones be crushed!—ploughed [under] the Temple building. —YERUSHALMI TAANIT 4:5 X

ISRAEL IN EXILE

When the sages of the Yerushalmi used the word "exile," they referred to a geographical category, namely, to any place outside the Land of Israel and to the condition of Jews living there. That entirely conventional—not even political—usage then reduced the dimension of exile to a single matter, leaving for others, in later times, to develop the spiritual notion that, with the destruction of the Temple, God went into exile from the world, and Israel from itself. So exile in the Talmud at hand does not carry the connotation of alienation and dislocation, except in a material sense. The lands outside the Holy Land suffered from cultic uncleanness. They were unclean in the way in which a corpse was unclean, and, it follows, outside the Land lay death, inside it, life; outside, graveyards, inside, the life of the people.

That accounts for the punctilious discussion of whether and under what conditions priests (kohanim), who were to maintain cultic cleanness when they served in the Temple, might even leave the country.

A priest came to Rabbi Hanina. He said to him: What is the law as to going to Tyre to carry out a religious duty, namely, to perform the rite of *halisah* or to enter into levirate marriage?

He said to him: Your brother went abroad. Blessed is the Omnipresent, who has smitten him. And now you want to do the same thing? There is one who wishes to say that this is what he said to him: Your brother left the bosom of his mother and embraced the bosom of a gentile woman, and blessed is He who smote him! And now you wish to do the same thing?

Simeon bar Ba came to Rabbi Hanina. He said to him: Write a letter of recommendation for me, since I am going abroad to make a living. He said to him: Tomorrow I'm going to your ancestors and they are going to say to me: That single planting [which gave us] pleasure which we had in the Land of Israel have you permitted to go abroad! [Hence I cannot approve your leaving the Holy Land.] —YERUSHALMI MOED QATAN 3:1 II

The intense land-centeredness of the Yerushalmi far transcended considerations only of the cult. For, as we see, the Land

fell into a different category altogether from all other lands. In the Land of Israel the Messiah would make his appearance. In the Land of Israel life, until then, was to be lived. The calendar, regulating the holy seasons in line with the movement of the moon and the sun, was governed only by the sightings taken in the Holy Land.

They do not intercalate the year abroad, and if they did so, it is not intercalated. Now you see that in Galilee they do not intercalate. So [it hardly seems likely] that they intercalate abroad.

The point is this: In Galilee they do not intercalate the year. Yet if they did so, it indeed is intercalated. Abroad they do not intercalate, and if they did so, it is *not* intercalated. This rule applies when they are able to intercalate in the Land of Israel. But if they are unable to intercalate in the Land of Israel, then they do intercalate the year abroad. Jeremiah intercalated the year abroad. Ezekiel intercalated the year abroad. Barukh ben Neriah intercalated the year abroad.

Rabbi sent three letters with Rabbi Isaac and Rabbi Nathan. In one he wrote: To his holiness, Hananiah [a Babylonian rabbi]. And in one he wrote: The lambs that you have left behind have become rams. [We in the Holy Land are your equal.] And in one he wrote: If you do not accept our authority, go out to the thorny wilderness, and there be the slaughterer [of the sacrifice], with Nehunyon, the sprinkler [of blood upon the altar]. [We exercise authority over you.]

[Hananiah] read the first and did obeisance, the second and did likewise. But when he read the third, he wanted to disgrace the messengers. They said to him: You cannot, for you have already treated us with honor.

Rabbi Isaac stood up and read in the Torah: These are the festivals of Hananiah, the nephew of Rabbi Joshua. He said: These are the festivals of the Lord Leviticus 23:2 is what is written. He replied: They are with us [in Israel, and your intercalation of the festivals is invalid, since you have intercalated abroad, and that is not to be done].

Rabbi Nathan arose and read in the prophetic passage: For from Babylonia will Torah go forth, and the word of the Lord from

Nehar Peqod. They said to him: [It is written:] For from Zion will Torah go forth, and the word of the Lord from Jerusalem Isaiah 2:3. He said to them: [The Torah is] with us. [Your decrees are not authoritative.]

[Hananiah] went and complained about them to Rabbi Judah ben Bathera in Nisibis. He said to them: "After them ... after them ..." [meaning, one must accept the authority of the majority]. He said to him: Do I not know what is over there? What tells me that they are masters of calculating the calendar like me? Since they are not so well informed as I am in calculating the calendar, let them listen to what I say. [He replied:] And since they [now] are masters of calculation as much as you, you must listen to them.

He rose up and mounted his horse. Places which he reached, he reached, [and there he retracted his intercalation,] and the ones he did not reach observed the holy days in error.

It is written: [These are the words of the letter which Jeremiah the prophet sent from Jerusalem] to the rest of the elders of the exiles Jeremiah 29:1. Said the Holy One, blessed be He: The elders of the exile are most valuable to Me. [Yet] more beloved to Me is the smallest circle which is located in the Land of Israel, more than a Great Sanhedrin located outside of the Land. It is written: ... and the craftsmen and the smiths, one thousand 2 Kings 24:16 — and you say this! [Namely, how can you say that the smallest circle in the Land is more beloved than an important Sanhedrin abroad? The craftsman and smiths are assumed to be disciples of sages, and they are many and important in Babylonia.] —YERUSHALMI NEDARIM 6:8 III

ISRAEL AND THE NATIONS

Israel endures. Its task among the nation is to represent the Torah honorably, as illustrated in the passage immediately following; and to remain loyal to the one God, who created Heaven and earth and gave the Torah. Whatever the nations do to Israel, whether in the Land of Israel or otherwise, Israel remains firm in its loyalty to, and love of, God.

The Government sent two officers to study Torah with Rabban Gamaliel. They studied with him Scripture, Mishnah, Talmud, laws and lore. At the end they said to him: The whole of your Torah is beautiful and praiseworthy, except for these two rules which you state: **An Israelite girl should not serve as a midwife to a gentile woman ... but a gentile woman may serve as a midwife to an Israelite girl. An Israelite girl should not give suck to the child of a gentile woman, but a gentile woman may give suck to the child of an Israelite girl when it is by permission** Mishnah Abodah Zarah 2:1 [which is to say:] What is stolen from an Israelite is prohibited, but from a gentile is permitted.

At that moment Rabban Gamaliel issued a decree against stealing from a gentile, declaring it forbidden because of the profanation of God's name.

[In the case of] An ox belonging to an Israelite which gored an ox belonging to a gentile—[the Israelite owner] is exempt. And [in the case of] one belonging to a gentile which gored one belonging to an Israelite—whether it is harmless or an attested danger, [the gentile owner] pays full damages Mishnah Baba Qamma 4:3 This matter, too, we cannot concede [to be just].

Even so, they had not reached the Ladder of Tyre [a spot nearby] before they had forgotten everything they learned. – YERUSHALMI BABA QAMMA 4:3 III

When Israel obeys God's will, the pagans and their gods come to no account. When Israel disobeys God's will, the pagan kingdoms flourish. So when Solomon married Pharaoh's daughter, Rome was founded.

Saturnalia means "hidden hatred" [SIN'AH TEMUNAH]: [The Lord] hates, takes vengeance, and punishes. This is in accordance with the following verse: Now Esau [=Rome] hated Jacob [=Israel] Genesis 27:41. Said Rabbi Isaac ben Rabbi Eleazar: In Rome they call it Esau's Saturnalia.

Kratesis [a Roman festival] is the day on which the Romans seized power. Now has this opinion already been assigned [to Kalends, another Roman festival by Yohanan who said that the day on which Rome seized power is Kalends, not Kratesis]? Said Rabbi

Yose ben Rabbi Bun: It [celebrates] the second time [that Rome seized power]. Said Rabbi Levi: It is the day on which Solomon intermarried with the family of Pharaoh Necho, king of Egypt. On that day [the angel] Michael came down and thrust a reed into the sea, and pulled up muddy alluvium, and this was turned into a huge pot, and this was the great city of Rome. On the day on which Jeroboam set up the two golden calves, Remus and Romulus came and built two huts in the city of Rome. On the day on which Elijah disappeared, a king was appointed in Rome: There was no king in Edom, a deputy was king 1 Kings 22:48. —YERUSHALMI ABODAH ZARAH 1:2 IV

Israel's continuing task is to resist the oppression of the gentiles and to sanctify God's name in public — even at the cost of martyrdom.

When the government first became oppressive, Rabbi Yannai gave instructions that the people might plough one time. There was an apostate to idolatry, who transgressed the laws of the Seventh Year. When [Rabbi Yannai] saw them throw up the ploughed clods, he said to them: Oh! that perversion of the law! You have been given permission to plough [in the Sabbatical Year, only on account of the edicts of the government], but have you been permitted to throw up the ploughed clods?

[As to Yannai's permitting the people to plough in the Seventh Year,] said Rabbi Jacob bar Zabedi: I asked before Rabbi Abbahu: Did not Zeira and Rabbi Yohanan in the name of Rabbi Yannai say, [or] Rabbi Yohanan in the name of Rabbi Simeon ben Yehosedeq: They voted in the upper room of the house of Nitzeh in Lud. In regard to the Torah, how do we know that if an idolater should tell an Israelite to transgress any one of all of the religious duties which are stated in the Torah, except for idolatry, fornication, and murder, that he should transgress and not be put to death. . . . ?

Now that rule applies to some matter which is done in private. But if it is a matter of public desecration, then even for the most minor religious duty, one should not obey him. [So how could Yannai have permitted the people to plough in the Seventh Year?] For example, there is the case of Papus and Lulianos, his brother, to whom they gave water in a colored glass flask [bearing an idol's name], and they did not accept it from them.

[Yannai] said: [The case is different here, for] they do not have in mind to force the Jews to commit apostasy [which is not the issue], but solely to pay taxes. [In such a case it is permitted publicly to violate the laws of the Torah, except for idolatry, fornication, and murder.]

How many must be present for the case to involve public desecration? Rabbis of Caesarea say: Ten [people constitute a public setting], as it is written: I will be sanctified among the people of Israel [and ten Israelites are required to form a *minyan* for prayer] Leviticus 22:32.

They saw Rabbi Bina the Younger running after an ass on the Sabbath [at the instance of idolaters]. Rabbi Yonah and Rabbi Yose gave instructions to bake bread for Ursicinus on the Sabbath. Said Rabbi Mana: I asked before Rabbi Yonah, Father, now did not Rabbi Zeira, Rabbi Yohanan in the name of Rabbi Yannai, Rabbi Jeremiah, Rabbi Yohanan in the name of Rabbi Simeon ben Yehosedeq say: They voted in the upper room of the house of Nitzeh, etc. [So how can you permit Jews to bake bread in public on the Sabbath?] [It was permitted because Ursicinus] did not intend to force them to apostasize; he intended only to eat warm bread.

How many must be present for the case to involve public desecration? Rabbis of Caesarea say: Ten, as it is written, I will be sanctified among the people of Israel Leviticus 22:32.

Rabbi Abuna raised the question to Rabbi Ami: As to idolaters, what is the law regarding their being commanded to sanctify the Name? He said to him: I will be sanctified among the people of Israel Leviticus 22:32. Israelites are commanded to sanctify God's Name, and idolaters are not commanded to sanctify God's Name.

Rabbi Nisi in the name of Rabbi Eleazar derived the same rule from the following: In this matter may the Lord pardon your servant [Naaman]: [when my master goes into the house of Rimmon to worship there, ... and I bow myself in the house of Rimmon, the Lord pardon your servant in this matter] 2 Kings 5:18. This indicates that Israelites are commanded concerning the sanctification of God's Name [and they must not practice idolatry, as in the cited instance], but idolaters are not commanded concerning the sanctification of God's Name.

Rabbi Ba bar Zamina was employed in sewing clothes by someone in Rome. [The Roman] brought him carrion meat. He said to him: Eat. He said to him: I am not going to eat. He said to him: Eat, or I'll kill you. He said to him: If you want to kill me, kill me, but I'm not going to eat carrion meat. He said to him: Who told you [that my intention was to test you], for had you eaten the meat, I would have killed you. If you are going to be a Jew, be a Jew. If you are going to be a Roman, be a Roman ["Aramean"]. Said Rabbi Mana: Had Rabbi Ba bar Zamina heard the teaching of the rabbis [who ruled that it is permissible to transgress in private], he would have eaten in this case. —YERUSHALMI SANHEDRIN 3:5 II

3

God's Condition

GOD CARED FOR HUMANITY. The Hebrew Scriptures — now "the whole Torah"— told the story of that long love. The age at hand tried not only Israel but God as well. The no-gods of the great empires enjoyed the glory of the world, while the one true God who had revealed Himself to Israel suffered the fate of Israel. Who, after all, could take seriously the pretension of a god who had lost (or permitted the destruction of) the temple that had fed him and the priests that had served him? In the view of the sages of the Yerushalmi, God's condition in Heaven presented the counterpart to Israel's on earth. But there was an important difference.

The sages affirmed that God governed. What happened therefore expressed God's will and wish. God cared. God's will therefore responded to humanity's heart and soul. God responded to what people did, but also to how they felt: their yearnings and hopes mattered even on high. Only Israel, having received the Torah, might want the things that God truly wished. In the end, therefore, Israel's condition would change, as God's will responded to Israel's rebirth and renewal in true conciliation.

Meanwhile, the condition of the world corresponded to the catastrophe of Israel: God was alien to the creation in which no-gods, not God, were served.

GOD AND THE NO-GODS

These three selections set forth a condition, a question, and a response. God is truth; the gods are lies (the first extract). God is sole ruler (the second extract). Then why does God suffer idolatry to endure, and even prosper, in the world God created and governs? The answer, in the third extract, derives from an extended discussion, spread over the Mishnah, the Tosefta, and the Talmud.

What is the seal of the Holy One, blessed be He? Rabbi Bibi in the name of Rabbi Reuben: It is *emet* ["Truth"]. What is the meaning of "Truth?" Said Rabbi Bun: It is that He is the living God and the everlasting king Jeremiah 10:10.

Said Rabbi Simeon ben Laqish: An *alef* [the first letter of *emet*] stands at the beginning of the alphabet, a *mem* [the middle letter] stands at the middle, and a *tav* [the final letter] stands at the end [of the alphabet] to indicate I am the first—for I did not accept dominion by anyone else's authority. And besides Me there is no god—for I have no colleague. And I am the last—for in the end I shall not hand over [dominion] to another Isaiah 44:6 [order transposed]. —YERUSHALMI SANHEDRIN 1:1 IV

And the sages say: Only [an idol] that has in its hand a staff, bird, or sphere is prohibited Mishnah Abodah Zarah 3:1. A staff— for [this implies] it rules the world with [a staff]. A bird—My hand has found like a nest the wealth of the peoples Isaiah 10:14. A sphere—for the world is shaped like a sphere.

Said Rabbi Yonah: When Alexander of Macedon wanted, he could wing upward, and he would go up. He traveled upward until he saw the world as a sphere and the sea as a dish. That is why they represent the world as a sphere in the hand [of an idol]. So let them depict a dish in [the idol's] hand too? [The idol] does not rule over the ocean. But the Holy One, blessed be He, rules over sea and land, saving [those who are in need] at sea and saving [those in need] on dry land.

Rabbi Zeira son of Rabbi Abbahu expounded the following verse in the presence of Rabbi Eleazar: Happy is he whose help is the God of Jacob, whose hope is in the Lord his God Psalms 146:5. Now what is written immediately thereafter? Who made heaven and earth, the sea and all that is in them Psalms 146:6. Now what has one thing to do with the other? But a mortal king has a patron [to whom he is subservient]. In this realm he does not [truly] rule. Is it possible that he [really] rules in some other? And if you would claim that there is the cosmocrator [who rules the world], he rules only on dry land, but not on the sea. But the Holy One, blessed be He, is not so. He is ruler by sea and ruler by land. And not only so, but if there is a sword hanging over the neck of a man, the Holy One, blessed be He, saves him. That is the meaning of what Moses said: He delivered me from the sword of Pharaoh Exodus 18:4. What is written here is, from the sword — meaning: even if a sword is hanging over above one's neck, the Holy One, blessed be He, saves him from it. —YERUSHALMI ABODAH ZARAH 3:1 III

They asked the sages in Rome: If [God] is not in favor of idolatry, why does he not wipe it away? They said to them: If people worshipped something of which the world had no need, He certainly would wipe it away. But lo, the people worship the sun, moon, stars, and planets. Now do you think He is going to wipe out his world because of idiots? They said to them: If so, let Him destroy something of which the world has no need, and leave something that the world needs! They said to them: Then we should strengthen the hands of those who worship [what is not destroyed], for then they would say: Now you know full well that they are gods, for lo, they were not wiped out.

Philosophers asked the sages in Rome: [If God] is not in favor of idolatry, why does he not wipe it away? They said to them: [If] people worshipped something of which the world had no need, he certainly would wipe it away. But lo, people worship the sun, moon, and stars. Now do you think he is going to wipe out his world because of idiots? Mishnah Abodah Zarah 4:7. [But let the world follow its accustomed way, and the idiots who behave ruinously will ultimately come and give a full account of

themselves.] If one has stolen seeds for planting, are they not ultimately going to sprout? If one has had sexual relations with a
married woman, will she not ultimately give birth? But let the
world follow its accustomed way, and the idiots who behave
ruinously will ultimately come and give a full account of themselves Tosefta Abodah Zarah 6:7.

Said Rabbi Zeira: If it were written: Those who worship are
like them, there would be no problem. Are those who worship the
sun like the sun, those who worship the moon like the moon?! But
this is what is written: Those who make them are like them; so are
all who trust in them Psalms 115:8. Said Rabbi Mana: If it were written: Those who worship them are like them, it would pose no
problem whatsoever. For it also is written: Then the moon will be
confounded, and the sun ashamed Isaiah 24:23.

Rabbi Nahman in the name of Rabbi Mana: Idolatry is destined in the end to come and spit in the face of those that worship
idols, and it will bring them to shame and cause them to be nulli-
fied from the world. Now what is the scriptural basis for that
statement? All worshippers of images will be put to shame, who
make their boast in worthless idols Psalms 97:7. Rabbi Nahman in the
name of Rabbi Mana: Idolatry is destined, in time, to come and
to bow down before the Holy One, blessed be He, and then be nul-
lified from the world. What is the scriptural basis for that
statement? [All worshippers of images will be put to shame . . .;] all
gods bow down before Him Psalms 97:7. —YERUSHALMI ABODAH ZARAH 4:1

GOD AND ISRAEL'S IDOLS

*Israel has written a long history of idolatry, from the very moment
at which the Torah was revealed onward. But at special times
individuals made a large contribution to Israel's ongoing apostasy,
Jeroboam and Ahab, for example.*

**Three kings and four ordinary folk have no portion in the
world to come. Three kings: Jeroboam, Ahab, and Manasseh.**
And all of [the three kings] invented new kinds of transgression.

Now what did Jeroboam do? It was because he made two
golden calves. And is it not so that the Israelites had made any

number of golden calves [so what was new about this]? Rabbi
Simeon ben Yohai taught: Thirteen golden calves did the Israelites
make, and there was one which was common property for all of
them. What is the scriptural basis for this statement? [And he
received the gold at their hand, and fashioned it with a graving
tool, and made a molten calf; and they said:] These are your gods,
O Israel [who brought you up out of the land of Egypt] Exodus 32:4.
Lo, they were for the twelve tribes. [Even when they had made for
themselves a molten calf and said:] This is your god [who brought
you up out of Egypt, and had committed great blasphemies]
Nehemiah 9:18. [The reference to This is your god] indicates the [thir-
teenth] one which was common property for all.

What did Ahab do? He would adorn himself every day and
get up before Hiel, commander of his army [1 Kings 16:34], and he
would say to him: How much am I worth today? And he would say
to him: Thus and so. Then he would take the amount [that he was
said to be worth] and set it apart for an idol. That is in line with the
following: [Ahab said to Elijah: Have you found me, O my enemy?
He answered: I have found you,] because you have sold yourself
to do what is evil in the sight of the Lord 1 Kings 21:20. —YERUSHALMI
SANHEDRIN 10:2

Said Rabbi Yudan, father of Rabbi Mattenaiah: The intention of [a verse of] Scripture [such as is cited below] was only to
make mention of the evil traits of Israel. On the day of [the anoint-
ing of] our king [Jeroboam] the princes became sick with the heat
of wine; he stretched out his hand with mockers Hosea 7:5. On the
day on which Jeroboam began to reign over Israel, all Israel came
to him at dusk, saying to him: Rise up and make an idol. He said
to them: It is already dusk. I am partly drunk and partly sober, and
the whole people is drunk. But if you want, go and come back in
the morning. This is the meaning of the following Scripture: For
like an oven their hearts burn with intrigue; all night their anger
smolders[; in the morning it blazes like a flaming fire] Hosea 7:6.

All night their anger smolders; in the morning it blazes like
a flaming fire. In the morning they came to him. Thus did he say
to them: I know what you want. But I am afraid of your Sanhedrin,
lest it come and kill me. They said to him: We shall kill them. That

is the meaning of the following verse: All of them are hot as an oven. And they devour their rulers Hosea 7:7. [Concurring with this view,] Rabbi Levi said: They slew them. Thus do you read in Scripture [to prove that the princes became sick [HHL] means the princes killed [HLL]: If anyone is found slain [HLL] Deuteronomy 21:1.

Rabbi does not [concur. He maintains that] they removed them from their positions of power [but did not kill the Sanhedrin]. On the day of our king the princes became sick with the heat of wine — it was the day on which the princes became sick. What made them sick? It was the heat of the wine, for they were thirsting for wine. He stretched out his hand with the mockers — When he would see an honorable man, he would set up against him two mockers, who would say to him: Now which generation do you think is the most cherished of all generations? He would answer them: It was the generation of the wilderness [which received the Torah]. They would say to him: Now did they themselves not worship an idol? And he would answer them: Now do you think that, because they were cherished, they were not punished for their deed? And they would say to him: Shut up! The king wants to do exactly the same thing. Not only so, but [the generations of the wilderness] only made one [calf], while [the king] wants to make two. [So the king took counsel and made two calves of gold] and he set up one in Bethel, and the other he put in Dan 1 Kings 12:29.

The arrogance of Jeroboam is what condemned him decisively. Said Rabbi Yose bar Jacob: It was at the conclusion of a sabbatical year that Jeroboam began to rule over Israel. That is the meaning of the verse: [And Moses commanded them.] At the end of every seven years, at the set time of the year of release, at the feast of booths, when all Israel comes to appear before the Lord your God at the place which He will choose, you shall read this law before all Israel in their hearing Deuteronomy 31:10-11.

Jeroboam said: I shall be called upon to read [the Torah, as Scripture requires]. If I get up and read first, they will say to me: The king of the place [of the gathering, namely, Jerusalem] comes first. And if I read second, it is disrespectful to me. And, if I do not read at all, it is a humiliation for me. And, finally, if I let the people go up, they will abandon me and go over to the side of Rehoboam the son of Solomon. That is the meaning of the following verse of Scripture: [And Jeroboam said in his heart: Now the kingdom will turn back to the house of David;] if this people go up to offer sacrifices in the house of the Lord at Jerusalem, then the heart of this people will turn again to their Lord, to Rehoboam, king of Judah, and they will kill me and return to Rehoboam, king of Judah 1 Kings 12:26-27.

What then did he do? He made two calves of gold 1 Kings 12:28, and he inscribed on their heart: . . . lest they kill you [as counsel to his successors]. He said: Let every king who succeeds me look upon them.

Said Rabbi Huna: [The wicked go astray from the womb, they err from their birth speaking lies. They have venom like the venom of a serpent, like the deaf adder that stops its ear so that it does not hear the voice of charmers] or of the cunning caster of spells Psalms 58:6. Whoever was associated with [Jeroboam] he cast a spell over him [in the sin of the bull-calves].

Said Rabbi Huna: [Hearken, O house of the king! For the judgment pertains to you; for you have been a snare at Mizpah, and a net spread upon Tabor.] And they have made deep the pit of Shittim[, but I will chastise all of them] Hosea 5:1-2. For [Jeroboam] deepened the sin. He said: Whoever explains [the meaning of what has been inscribed on the bull-calves] I shall kill.

Said Rabbi Abin bar Kahana: Also in regard to the Sabbaths and the festivals we find that Jeroboam invented them on his own. That is the meaning of the following verse: And Jeroboam appointed a feast on the fifteenth day of the eighth month like the feast that was in Judah, and he offered sacrifices upon the altar [; so he did in Bethel, sacrificing to the calves that he had made] 1 Kings 12:32. Thus he did in Bethel, having sacrifices made in a month that he made up on his own. This is as you read in Scripture: In addition to the Sabbaths of the Lord Leviticus 23:38. [So Jeroboam confused the people by establishing his own calendar for Bethel, thereby keeping the people from making pilgrimages to Jerusalem.] —YERUSHALMI ABODAH ZARAH 1:1 I

Not only did Jeroboam add to the apostasy by his inventions, he also enticed the people to idolatry by claiming that it was the easier mode of worship.

Once Jeroboam took up the reign over Israel, he began to entice Israel [toward idolatry], saying to them: Come and let us practice idolatrous worship. Idolatry is permissive. That is the meaning of the following verse of Scripture: [Because Syria with Ephraim and the son of Remaliah has devised evil against you, saying:] Let us go up against Judah and terrify it, and let us conquer it for ourselves and set up the son of Tabeel as king in the midst of it Isaiah 7:5-6.

Said Rabbi Abba: We have searched through the whole of Scripture and have found no instance in which his name was Tabeel. But [the meaning is that] he does good for those who serve him. The Torah has said: I chose him [the tribe of Levi] out of all the tribes of Israel to be My priest, to go up to My altar, to burn incense, to wear an ephod before Me 1 Samuel 2:28. And idolatry says: [He also made houses on high places], and appointed priests from the fringe element (MQSWT) of the people[, who were not of the Levites] 1 Kings 12:31.

Said Rabbi: Not from the thorns [QWSYM] that were among the people, but from the refuse [PSWLT] that was among the people. The Torah has said: You shall not let the fat of My feast remain until the morning Exodus 23:18. But idolatry has said: Bring your sacrifices every morning Amos 4:4.

The Torah has said: [When you offer a sacrifice of peace-offerings to the Lord, you shall offer it so that you may be accepted.] It shall be eaten the same day you offer it, or on the morrow[; and anything left over until the third day shall be burned with fire] Leviticus 19:5-6. And idolatry has said: . . . your tithes on the third day Amos 4:4.

The Torah has said: You shall not offer the blood of My sacrifice with leavened bread Exodus 23:18. And idolatry has said: Offer a sacrifice of thanksgiving of that which is leavened Amos 4:5.

The Torah has said: When you make a vow to the Lord, your God, you shall not be slack to pay for it[; for the Lord your God will surely require it of you, and it would be a sin in you. But if you refrain from vowing, it shall be no sin in you. You shall be careful to perform what has passed your lips, for you have voluntarily vowed to the Lord your God what you have promised with your mouth] Deuteronomy 23:22-24. And idolatry has said: And proclaim freewill offerings, publish them Amos 4:5. —YERUSHALMI ABODAH ZARAH 1:1 I

GOD, ISRAEL, AND THE NATIONS

Although Israel's own rulers enticed the Israelites to practice idolatry, the greatest prophet of the gentiles, Balaam, showed the way. He advised the enemies of Israel to weaken and destroy the people by winning them away from God. The principal message in the next selection is that through sexual intercourse with gentiles Israelites gave up their loyalty to God. It follows that Israel must avoid intermarriage with gentiles, so as to remain fully in God's service.

Now what did the evil Balaam do [to warrant losing his portion in the world to come]? It was because he gave advice to Balaq son of Zippor on how to cause Israel's downfall by the sword. He said to him: The God of this nation hates fornication. So offer up your daughters for fornication, and you will rule over them.

[Balaq] said to him: And will [the Moabites] listen to me [when I tell them to turn their daughters into whores]?

He said to him: Offer up your own daughter first, and they will see and then accept what you say to them.

That is in line with the following verse of Scripture: [And the name of the Midianite woman who was slain was Cozbi, the daughter of Zur,] who was the head of the people of a father's house in Midian Numbers 25:15.

What did they do? They built for themselves temples from Beth HaJeshimmon to the Snowy Mountain, and they set in them women selling various kinds of sweets. They put the old lady outside and the young girl inside. Now the Israelite would eat and drink, and one of them would go out to walk in the marketplace, and he would buy something from a stallkeeper. The old lady then would sell him the thing for whatever it was worth, and the young girl would say: Come on in and take it for still less. So it was on the first day, the second day, and the third day. And by then, she would say to him: From now on, you belong here. Come on in and choose whatever you like.

When he came in, [he found there] a flagon full of wine — Ammonite wine, which is very strong. And it serves as an aphrodisiac to the body, and its scent was enticing. (Now up to this time the wine of the gentiles had not been prohibited for Israelite use by reason of its being libation wine.) Now the girl would say to him:

Do you want to drink a cup of wine? And he would reply to her: Yes. So she gave him a cup of wine, and he drank it.

When he drank it, the wine would burn in him like the venom of a snake. Then he would say to her: Surrender yourself to me. She would say to him: Do you want me to surrender myself to you? And he would say: Yes. Then she took out an image of Peor from her bosom, and she said to him: Bow down to this, and I'll surrender myself to you. And he would say to her: Now am I going to bow down to an idol? And she would say to him: You don't really bow down to it, but you expose yourself to it. This is in line with that which the sages have said, He who exposes himself to Baal Peor—this is the appropriate manner of worshipping it; and he who tosses a stone at Merkolis—this is the appropriate manner of worshipping it.

[When he came in, he found] there a flagon full of wine— Ammonite wine, which is very strong. And it serves as an aphrodisiac to incite the body to passion, and its scent was enticing. (Now up to this time the wine of the gentiles had not been prohibited for Israelite use by reason of its being libation wine.) Now the girl would say to him: Do you want to drink a cup of wine? And he would reply to her: Yes. So she gave him a cup of wine, and he drank it.

When he drank it, the wine would burn in him like the venom of a snake. Then he would say to her: Surrender yourself to me. She would say to him: Separate yourself from the Torah of Moses, and I shall surrender myself to you. That is in line with the following verse of Scripture: Like grapes in the wilderness, I found Israel. Like the first fruits on the fig tree, in their first season, I saw your fathers. But they came to Baal Peor, and consecrated themselves to Baal, and became detestable like the thing they loved Hosea 9:10.

They became detested until they became detestable to their Father who is in Heaven. Said Rabbi Eleazar: Just as this nail— one cannot separate it from the door without a piece of wood, so it is not possible to separate from Peor with [the loss of] souls.

Subetah from Ulam hired out his ass to a gentile woman [to take her] to bow down to Peor. When they got to Peor's [temple], she said to him: Wait for me here, while I go in and worship Peor.

When she came out, he said to her: Wait for me here, until I go in and do just as you did. What did he do? He went in and defecated, and he wiped his behind on the nose of Peor. Everyone present praised him, and [it was said of him]: No one ever did it the way this one did!

Menahem of Gypta Arye was moving jugs. The chief of Peor came to him by night. What did he do? He took the spit and stood up against him, and [the chief] fled from him. He came to him the next night. Menahem said to him: How are you going to curse me? You are afraid of me! And he said to [Menahem]: I'm not going to curse you any more.

An officer came from overseas to bow down to Peor. He said to them: Bring me an ox, a ram, [and] a sheep to worship Peor. They said to him: You don't have to go to all that trouble. All you have to do is expose yourself to it. What did he do? He called up his troops, who beat them and broke their skulls with staves, and he said to them: Woe for you and for this big "mistake" of yours! It is written: And the Lord was angry at Israel, and the Lord said to Moses: Take all the chiefs of the people, and hang them in the sun before the Lord, [that the fierce anger of the Lord may turn away from Israel] Numbers 25:4.

[The officer said:] Appoint their heads as judges over them, and let them put the sinners to death toward the sun.

This is in line with the following verse of Scripture: And Moses said to the judges of Israel: Every one of you slay his men who have yoked themselves to Baal Peor Numbers 25:5. And how many are the judges of Israel? They are 78,600 [calculated as follows]: heads of thousands are 600, heads of hundreds are 6,000, head of troops of fifty are 12,000, head of troops of ten are 60,000. It thus turns out that the judges of Israel [heads of all units] are 78,600. [Moses] said to them: Each one of you kill two. So, in all, 157,200 were put to death.

And, behold, one of the people of Israel came and brought a Midianite woman to his family, in the sight of Moses [and in the sight of the whole congregation of the people of Israel, while they were weeping at the door of the tent of meeting Numbers 25:6. What is the meaning of in the sight of Moses? It was like someone who says: Here — right in your eye! [That one] said [to Moses]: Is your

Zipporah not Midianite, and are her feet not cloven? [Can it be that what is acceptable for you is not acceptable for me?] This one [Zipporah] is clean, but that one [my woman] is unclean?

Now Phineas was there. He said: Is there no man here who will kill him even at the expense of his life? Where are the lions? Judah is a lion's whelp; [from the prey, my son, you have gone up. He stooped down, he crouched as a lion, and as a lioness who dares to rouse him?] Genesis 49:9. [And of Dan he said:] Dan is a lion's whelp, [that leaps forth from Bashan] Deuteronomy 33:22. Benjamin is a ravenous wolf, [in the morning devouring the prey, and at even dividing the spoil] Genesis 49:27. When [Phineas] saw that no Israelite did a thing, forthwith Phineas stood up from his Sanhedrin seat and took a spear in his hand and put the iron head of it under his garment. He leaned on the wood [of the spear, so concealing its purpose] until he reached his door. When he came to his door, [those who answered] said to him: Whence and whither, Phineas? He said to them: Do you not agree with me that the tribe of Levi is near the tribe of Simeon under all circumstances? They said to him: Leave him alone. Maybe the separatists have permitted this matter [after all]!

When [Phineas] got in, the Holy One, blessed be He, did six miracles. The first miracle: It is the usual way [following intercourse, for a man and a woman] to separate from one another, but the angel of the Lord kept them stuck together. The second miracle: [Phineas] aimed the spear directly into the belly of the [Midianite] woman, so that the [Israelite] man's penis would stick out of her belly. (And this was on account of the scoffers, so that they should not go around saying: He too shouldered his way in and did what came naturally.) The third miracle: The angel sealed their lips, so that they could not cry out. The fourth miracle: They did not slip off the spear but remained in place [so that Phineas lifted them up on the spear]. The fifth miracle: The angel raised the lintel, so that both of them could go out [through the doorway, still impaled on the spear] on his shoulders. The sixth miracle: When he went out and saw the plague afflicting the people, what did [Phineas] do? He threw them down to the ground and stood and prayed. This is in line with the following verse of Scripture: Then Phineas stood up and interposed, and the plague was stayed Psalms 106:30.

Now when the Israelites came to take vengeance against Midian, they found Balaam ben Beor there. And what had he come to do? He had come to collect his salary for the twenty-four thousand Israelites who had died in Shittim on his account. Phineas said to him: You did not do what you said, and you also did not do Balaq's bidding. You did not do what you said, for He said to you: You shall not go with the messengers of Balaq, but you went along with them. And you did not do what Balaq said, for he said to you: Go and curse Israel, but you blessed them. So, for my part, I shall not withhold your salary! This is in line with that which is written in Scripture: Balaam also, the son of Beor, the soothsayer, the people of Israel killed with the sword among the rest of their slain Joshua 13:22.

What is the meaning of among the rest of their slain? That he was equal to all the other slain put together. Another interpretation: Among the rest of their slain — just as their slain no longer have substance, so he was of no substance. Another interpretation: Among the rest of their slain — For he hovered [in the air] over their slain, and Phineas showed him the [priestly] frontlet, and he fell down [to earth]. Another interpretation: Among the rest of their slain —This teaches that the Israelites paid him his salary in full and did not hold it back. —YERUSHALMI SANHEDRIN 10:2 VIII

GOD AND ISRAEL IN EXILE

The single most important point is that God shares the condition of Israel, has gone into exile with Israel, has lost the Temple along with Israel, mourns for Jerusalem, and suffers the pain of the people.

Said Rabbi Hanina son of Rabbi Abbahu: In the book of Rabbi Meir they found that it was written: The oracle concerning Dumah. One is calling to me from Seir, Watchman, what of the night? Watchman, what of the night? Isaiah 21:11.

Said Rabbi Yohanan: One is calling to me because of Seir. Said Rabbi Simeon ben Laqish: To me. From whence will there be a match for me? From Seir.

Said Rabbi Joshua ben Levi: If someone should say to you:

Where is your God? say to him: He is in a great city in Edom. What is the scriptural basis for this view? One is calling to me from Seir Isaiah 21:11.

It has been taught by Rabbi Simeon ben Yohai: To every place to which the Israelites went into exile, the presence of God went with them into exile. They were sent into exile to Egypt, and the presence of God went into exile with them. What is the scriptural basis for this claim? And there came a man of God to Eli, and said to him: Thus the Lord has said: I revealed myself to the house of your fathers when they were in Egypt subject to the house of Pharaoh 1 Samuel 2:27.

They were sent into exile to Babylonia, and the presence of God went into exile with them. What is the scriptural basis for this claim? Thus says the Lord, your Redeemer, the Holy One of Israel: For your sake, I shall send to Babylon and break down all the bars, and the shouting of the Chaldeans will be turned to lamentations Isaiah 43:14.

They were sent into exile into Media, and the presence of God went into exile with them. What is the scriptural basis for this claim? And I shall set My throne in Elam, and destroy their king and princes, says the Lord Jeremiah 49:38. And Elam means only Media, as it is said: And I saw in the vision; and when I saw, I was in Susa the capital, which is in the province of Elam; and I saw in the vision, and I was at the river Ulai Daniel 8:2.

They went into exile to Greece, and the presence of God went into exile with them. What is the scriptural basis for this claim? For I have bent Judah as My bow; I have made Ephraim its arrow. I will brandish your sons, O Zion, over your sons, O Greece, and wield you like a warrior's sword Zechariah 9:13.

They went into exile to Rome, and the presence of God went into exile with them. What is the scriptural basis for this claim? The oracle concerning Dumah. One is calling to me from Seir, Watchman, what of the night? Watchman, what of the night? Isaiah 21:11. —YERUSHALMI TAANIT 1:1 X

4

God and Israel: The Common Condition

TWO HUNDRED YEARS HAD PASSED from the closure of the Mishnah to the completion of the Yerushalmi. Much had changed. Roman power had receded from part of the world. Pagan rule had given way to the sovereignty of Christian emperors. The old order was cracking; the new order was not yet established. But from the perspective of Israel and its condition, the waiting went on. The interim from Temple to Temple was not differentiated. Whether conditions were less favorable or more favorable hardly made a difference. History stretched backward to a point of disaster, and forward to an unseen and incalculable time beyond the near horizon. Short of supernatural events, salvation was not in sight. Israel for its part lived under its own government, framed within the rules of sanctification, and constituted a holy society. But when would salvation come, and how could people even now hasten its arrival? These issues, in the nature of things, proved more pressing as the decades rolled by, becoming first one century, then another, while none knew how many more, and how much more, must still be endured. So the unredeemed state of Israel and the world, the uncertain fate of the individual—these framed and defined the context in which all issues necessarily took shape.

GOD AND ISRAEL

The principal issue was how to return to God, how to attain recon-
ciliation after the punishment and age of atonement represented
by the past several hundred years. Eager to avoid stirring up those
dormant fires that had led Israel to the battleground time and
again, the sages emphasized the favor enjoyed by Israel because
of its heritage of merit and holiness. These resources of strength
would serve, as much as the effort of the living generation, but with
better result. Accordingly, they spoke about the merits of the
patriarchs – merits that yet endured to protect Israel.

How long did the merit of the patriarchs endure [to protect
Israel]? Rabbi Tanhuma said in the name of Rabbi Hiyya the Great,
Bar Nahman stated in the name of Rabbi Berekhiah, Rabbi Helbo
in the name of Rabbi Ba bar Zabeda: Down to Joahaz. But the
Lord was gracious to them and had compassion on them
[because of His covenant with Abraham, Isaac, and Jacob, and
would not destroy them; nor has He cast them from His presence]
until now 2 Kings 13:23. Down to that time the merit of the patriarchs
endured.

Samuel said: Down to Hosea. Now I shall uncover her lewd-
ness in the sight of her lovers, and no man shall rescue her out of
My hand Hosea 2:12. Now man can only refer to Abraham, as you
say: Now then restore the man's wife; for he is a prophet, [and he
will pray for you, and you shall live. But if you do not restore her,
know that you will surely die, you, and all that are yours] Genesis 20:7.
And man can only refer to Isaac, as you say: [Rebekah said to the
servant,] Who is the man yonder, walking in the field to meet us?
[The servant said: It is my master. So she took her veil and
covered herself] Genesis 24:65. And man can refer only to Jacob, as
you say: [When the boys grew up, Esau was a skilful hunter, a man
of the field,] while Jacob was a quiet man [dwelling in tents] Genesis 25:27.

Rabbi Joshua ben Levi said: It was down to Elijah. And at
the time of the offering of the oblation, Elijah the prophet came
near and said: O Lord, God of Abraham, Isaac, and Israel, let it be
known this day that You are God in Israel, and that I am Your servant, [and that I have done all these things at Your word] 1 Kings 18:36.

Rabbi Yudan said: It was down to Hezekiah. Of the increase of his government and of peace there will be no end [upon the throne of David, and over his kingdom, to establish it, and to uphold it with justice and with righteousness from this time forth and for evermore. The zeal of the Lord of hosts will do this] Isaiah 9:6.

Said Rabbi Aha: The merit of the patriarchs endures forever [to protect Israel]. For the Lord your God is a merciful God; [He will not fail you or destroy you or forget the covenant with your fathers which He swore to them] Deuteronomy 4:31. This teaches that the covenant is made with the tribes.

Rabbi Yudan bar Hanan in the name of Rabbi Berekhiah: Said the Holy One, blessed be He, to Israel: My children, if you see the merit of the patriarchs declining, and the merit of the matriarchs growing feeble, go and cleave unto the trait of steadfast love. What is the scriptural basis for this statement? For the mountains may depart and the hills be removed, [but My steadfast love shall not depart from you and My covenant of peace shall not be removed, says the Lord, who has compassion on you] Isaiah 54:10.

For the mountains may depart — this refers to the merit of the patriarchs. And the hills be removed — this refers to the merit of the matriarchs. Henceforth: But My steadfast love shall not depart from you and My covenant of peace shall not be removed, says the Lord, who has compassion on you. —YERUSHALMI SANHEDRIN 10:1 VI

The merits of the patriarchs served as one path of return. And the death of the righteous also effected expiation, much as the sacrifices had in times past.

Said Rabbi Hiyya bar Ba: The sons of Aaron died on the first day of Nisan. And why is their death called to mind in connection with the Day of Atonement [Leviticus 16]? It is to indicate to you that just as the Day of Atonement effects expiation for Israel, so the death of the righteous effects atonement for Israel.

Said Rabbi Ba bar Bina: Why did the Scripture place the story of the death of Aaron side by side with the story of the red cow [Numbers 19, 20]? It is to teach you that just as the dirt of the red cow [mixed with water] effects atonement for Israel, so the death of the righteous effects atonement for Israel.

Said Rabbi Yudan ben Shalom: Why did the Scripture set the story of the death of Aaron side by side with the story of the breaking of the tablets? It is to teach you that the death of the righteous is as grievous before the Holy One, blessed be He, as the breaking of the tablets. —YERUSHALMI YOMA 1:1 V

Finally, through a most elaborate sequence of public facts, people could express their penitence and seek reconciliation. They endured the symbols of suffering, exile, and famine, hoping to avoid the actualities. They showed themselves humble and accepting. These three — the merits of the patriarchs, the expiation in the death of the righteous, and the participation in the symbols of suffering — served to form Israel into the living model of the Temple. They offered themselves as sacrifices.

The manner of fasting: how [was it done]? They bring forth the ark into the street of the town and put wood ashes on the ark, the head of the patriarch, and the head of the head of the court. And each person puts ashes on his head. The eldest among them makes a speech of admonition: Our brothers, concerning the people of Nineveh it is not said, And God saw their sackcloth and their fasting, but And God saw their deeds, for they repented from their evil way Jonah 3:10. And in prophetic tradition it is said: Rend your heart and not your garments Joel 2:13.

Said Rabbi Hiyya bar Ba: And why do they go out into the street of the town? It is as if to say: Consider us as if we had gone into exile before You. Said Rabbi Joshua ben Levi: It is because they prayed in private and were not answered. Therefore they go out and make the matter public.

Said Rabbi Hiyya bar Ba: And why do they bring the ark out into the street? It is as if to say: This one precious object that we had — our sins have caused it to be disgraced. Rabbi Huna the Elder, of Sepphoris, said: Our forefathers covered it with gold, and we covered it with dirt.

Said Rabbi Jacob, the Southerner: And why do they sound the trumpets? It is as if to say: Consider us as if we are like a beast before You.

Said Rabbi Levi: And why do they go forth among the graves? It is as if to say: Consider us as if we were dead before You.

Said Rabbi Tanhuma: And in the case of all of them: If we are liable for the death penalty, lo, we are dead. If we are liable to exile, lo, we are exiled. If it is to famine, lo, we are fasting.

And they put wood ashes on the ark. It is in line with this verse: When he calls to Me, I will answer him; I will be with him in trouble, I will rescue him and honor him Psalms 91:15.

Said Rabbi Zeira: Whenever I see them doing this, my body trembles.

In the days of Rabbi Ila they would leave the ark out and go into [their houses]. Rabbi Zeira said to them: And has it not been taught: And they did not change guards for it. One person sits and watches it all day long Tosefta Taanit 1:8.

Rabbi Yudan ben Rabbi Manasseh and Rabbi Samuel bar Nahman. One said: [They put on dirt] in order to call to mind the merit of Abraham. The other said: [They do so] in order to call to mind the merit of Isaac [at the binding of Isaac].

He who holds that it is to call to mind the merit of Abraham says that it may be either dirt or wood ash, in line with the verse: I who am but dust and ashes Genesis 18:27. He who said it was so as to call to mind the merit of Isaac says that it must be ashes alone. They envision the ashes of Isaac as if they were piled on the altar.

When Rabbi Judah bar Pazzi would go forth to a fast, he would call before them: O our brethren! To whomever the beadle [of the synagogue] has not come, let him take dust and put it on his head.

And on the head of the patriarch. Said Rabbi Tahalipa of Caesarea: It is so as to make the matter known. One who degrades himself is not the same as one who is degraded by others. It is written: Let the bridegroom leave his room, and the bride her chamber Joel 2:16. The bridegroom leave his room—this refers to the ark. And the bride her chamber—this refers to the Torah.

Another interpretation: The bridegroom leave his room—this refers to the patriarch. And the bride her chamber—this refers to the head of the court.

Rabbi Helbo said to Rabbi Yudan the Patriarch: Come out with us, and what is painful to you will pass. [If the patriarch comes out with us to a public fast, the prayers will be answered. Otherwise we cannot properly carry out the rite.] Said Rabbi Yose: That is to say that these fasts that we carry out—they are not really fasts. Why not? Because the patriarch is not with us [and we cannot carry out the rite in the proper way]. —YERUSHALMI TAANIT 2:1 I

REPENTANCE

Above all repentance served as the road back to God, the way to overcome sin. No sin could prove too great for the power of repentance to secure forgiveness. This fact is shown in the story of how even the arch-idolater of Israel, Manasseh, in the end found forgiveness when he repented of his sins.

And it is written: Moreover Manasseh shed very much innocent blood, till he had filled Jerusalem from one end to another, [besides the sin which he made Judah to sin so that they did what was evil in the sight of the Lord] 2 Kings 21:16. Now is it possible for human beings to fill up the whole of Jerusalem with innocent blood from one end to another? [Not under ordinary circumstances,] but he killed Isaiah, who was equal to Moses, as it is written concerning him: With him I speak mouth to mouth, [clearly, and not in dark speech; and he beholds the form of the Lord. Why then were you not afraid to speak against My servant Moses? Numbers 12:8. And it is written: The Lord spoke to Manasseh and his people, but they gave no heed. Therefore the Lord brought upon them the commanders of the army of the king [of Assyria], who took Manasseh with hooks [and bound him with fetters of bronze and brought him to Babylon] 2 Chronicles 33:10-11.

What is with hooks? [They took him] in handcuffs. Said Rabbi Levi: They made him a mule of bronze and they put him in it, and they made a fire under it. When he began to feel pain, [there was] not a single idol in the world, on the name of which he did not call. When he realized that it did him no good, he said: I remember that my father would read to me this verse in the synagogue: When you are in tribulation, and all these things come upon you in the latter days, you will return to the merciful God; He will not fail you or destroy you or forget the covenant with your fathers which He swore to them Deuteronomy 4:30-31. Lo, I shall call upon Him. If He answers me, well and good, and if not, lo, all ways are the same [and no good].

Now all the ministering angels went and closed the windows, so that the prayer of Manasseh should not reach upward to the Holy One, blessed be He. The ministering angels were saying before the Holy One, blessed be He: Lord of the world, a man who worshipped idols and put up an image in the Temple – are you going to accept him back as a penitent? He said to them: If I do not accept him back as a penitent, lo, I shall lock the door before all penitents.

What did the Holy One, blessed be He, do? He made an opening [through the heavens] under His throne of glory and listened to his supplication. That is in line with the following verse of Scripture: He prayed to Him, and God received his entreaty ['TR] and heard his supplication and brought him again [to Jerusalem into his kingdom. Then Manasseh knew that the Lord was God] 2 Chronicles 33:13. Said Rabbi Eleazar ben Rabbi Simeon: In Arabia they call that "breaking through" [HTRTH], "supplication" ['TRTH].

And they brought him again to Jerusalem into his kingdom – with what did they bring him back? Samuel bar Buna in the name of Rabbi Aha: They brought him back with the wind. This is in line with that which you say: He brings back the wind.

And Manasseh knew that the Lord was God – at that moment Manasseh said: There truly is justice and there truly is a judge. —YERUSHALMI SANHEDRIN 10:2 VII

Speaking of Israel as a whole, Eliezer and Joshua, who lived at the end of the first century, maintained that the one way in which Israel would be redeemed would be through repentance.

Rabbi Eliezer says: If the Israelites do not repent, they will not be redeemed forever, since it is said, For thus says the Lord God, the Holy One of Israel: In returning and rest you shall be saved; in quietness and in trust shall be your strength. And you would not Isaiah 30:15.

Rabbi Joshua said to [Rabbi Eliezer]: And is it so, that if Israel should stand and not repent, they will not be redeemed forever? Rabbi Eliezer said to him: The Holy One, blessed be He, will appoint over them a king as harsh as Haman, and forthwith they will repent and so will be redeemed. What is the scriptural basis for this view? Alas! that day is so great there is none like it; it is a time of distress for Jacob; yet he shall be saved out of it Jeremiah 30:7.

Rabbi Joshua said to him: And lo, it is written: For thus says the Lord: You were sold for nothing, and you shall be redeemed without money Isaiah 52:3. [Meaning, redemption is without preconditions.] How does Rabbi Eliezer deal with the cited verse? It [presupposes] repentance, as Scripture has said: He took a bag of money with him Proverbs 7:20.

Rabbi Joshua said to him: And lo, it is written: I am the Lord; in its time I shall hasten it Isaiah 60:22. How does Rabbi Eliezer deal with this verse? It speaks of repentance, as it says: And now, Israel, what does the Lord your God require of you, but to fear the Lord your God, to walk in all His ways, to love Him, to serve the Lord your God with all your heart and with all your soul Deuteronomy 10:12.

Rabbi Aha in the name of Rabbi Joshua ben Levi: If you have merit, I shall hasten it, and if not, it will come only in its time. — YERUSHALMI TAANIT 1:1 VII

Moreover, no mode or form of atonement worked without repentance.

Said Rabbi Levi: What is the meaning of slow to anger? It means, "distant from wrath." It may be compared to a king who had two tough legions. The king said: If they dwell here with me in the metropolis, if the city-folk anger me, they will put them down [with force]. But lo, I shall send them a long way away, so that if the city-folk anger me, while I am yet summoning the legions, the people will appease me, and I shall accept their plea. Likewise the Holy One, blessed be He, said: Anger and wrath are angels of destruction. Lo, I shall send them a long way away, so that if Israel angers Me, while I am summoning them to Me, Israel will repent, and I shall accept their repentance. That is in line with the following verse of Scripture: They come from a distant land, from the end of the heavens, the Lord and the weapons of His indignation, to destroy the whole earth Isaiah 13:5.

Said Rabbi Isaac: And not only so, but He locks the gate before them. That is in line with what is written: The Lord has opened His armory and brought out the weapons of His wrath Jeremiah 50:25. While He is yet opening the armory, while He is yet occupied, His mercy draws near. —YERUSHALMI TAANIT 2:1 XI

Rabbi Mattiah ben Heresh asked Rabbi Eleazar ben Azariah: Have you heard of the four types of atonement that Rabbi Ishmael used to expound? He said to him: They are three, besides [the requirement of] an act of repentance. [These are the three types:] One Scripture says: Return, O faithless children, says the Lord Jeremiah 3:14. And yet another verse of Scripture says: For on this day shall atonement be made for you, to cleanse you; from all your sins you shall be clean before the Lord Leviticus 16:30. [So one verse recommends repentance, and the other grants absolution unconditionally.]

And one verse of Scripture says: Then I will punish their transgression with the rod and their iniquity with scourges Psalms 89:33. And yet another verse of Scripture says: Surely this iniquity will not be forgiven you till you die, says the Lord God of Hosts Isaiah 22:14. Now how are these verses to be reconciled [since they speak of punishment and forgiveness on the one side, and the impossibility of atonement except through death on the other]?

[If] one has violated a positive commandment but repented, he does not even leave the place before he is [wholly] forgiven. Concerning such a person the verse of Scripture says: Return, O faithless children. [If] one has violated a negative commandment and repented forthwith, the act of repentance suspends the punishment, and the Day of Atonement effects atonement for him. In such a case the Scripture states: For on this day shall atonement be made for you. [If] one has violated a commandment involving extirpation or the death penalty inflicted by a court, and has done so deliberately, repentance and the Day of Atonement effect atonement in part, and suffering effects atonement in part. Concerning such a person, the verse of Scripture states: Then I will punish their transgression with the rod, and their iniquity with scourges.

But as to him through whose action the Name of Heaven has been disgraced, repentance has not the power to suspend punishment, nor does the Day of Atonement have the power to effect atonement, nor does suffering have the power to wipe away the guilt. But repentance and the Day of Atonement suspend the punishment, along with suffering; the man's death wipes away the sin. Concerning such a person does Scripture make the statement: Surely this iniquity will not be forgiven you till you die. Thus we have learned the fact that death wipes away [guilt and sin]. — YERUSHALMI SHEBUOT 1:6 II

SALVATION

The messianic salvation thus depended on the repentance of Israel. The coming of the Messiah depended not on historical action but on moral regeneration, as shown in the last selection. From a force that moved Israelites to take up weapons on the battlefield, the messianic hope and yearning were transformed into motives for spiritual regeneration and ethical behavior. The energies released in the messianic fervor were then linked to rabbinical government, through which Israel would form the godly society.

When we reflect that the message — If you want it, He too wants it to be — comes in a generation confronting a dreadful disappointment, its full weight and meaning become clear. The advent of the Messiah will not be heralded by the actions of a pagan king. Whoever relies upon the salvation of a gentile is going to be disappointed. Israel's salvation depends wholly upon Israel itself. Two things follow. First, the Jews were made to take up the burden of guilt for their own sorry situation. But, second, they also gained not only responsibility for, but also power over, their fate. They could do something about salvation, just as their sins had brought about their tragedy.

Sages insisted the Messiah would come in a process extending over a long period of time, thus not imposing a caesura upon the existence of the nation and disrupting its ordinary life. Accordingly, the Yerushalmi treats the messianic hope as something gradual, to be worked toward, not a sudden cataclysmic event. That conception was fully in accord with the notion that the everyday deeds of people formed a pattern continuous with the salvific history of Israel.

The oracle concerning Dumah. One is calling to me from Seir, Watchman, what of the night? Watchman, what of the night? Isaiah 21:11. The Israelites said to Isaiah: O our Rabbi, Isaiah, what will come for us out of this night?

He said to them: Wait for me, until I can present the question. Once he had asked the question, he came back to them. They said to him: Watchman, what of the night? What did the Guardian of the ages tell you? He said to them: The watchman says: Morning comes; and also the night. If you will inquire, inquire; come back again Isaiah 21:12.

They said to him: Also the night? He said to them: It is not what you are thinking. But there will be morning for the righteous, and night for the wicked; morning for Israel and night for idolaters. They said to him: When? He said to them: Whenever you want, He too wants [it to be] — if you want it, He wants it.

They said to him: What is standing in the way? He said to them: Repentance: Come back again.

Rabbi Aha in the name of Rabbi Tanhuma ben Rabbi Hiyya: If Israel repents for one day, forthwith the son of David will come. What is the scriptural basis? Today, if you would hearken to His voice Psalms 95:7. —YERUSHALMI TAANIT 1:1 IX

Salvation is linked to keeping the law.

One time Rabbi Hiyya the Elder and Rabbi Simeon ben Halafta were walking in the valley of Arabel at daybreak. They saw that the light of the morning star was breaking forth. Said Rabbi Hiyya the Elder to Rabbi Simeon ben Halafta: Son of my master, this is what the redemption of Israel is like — at first, little by little, but in the end it will go along and burst into light. What is the scriptural basis for this view? Rejoice not over me, O my enemy; when I fall, I shall rise; when I sit in darkness, the Lord will be a light to me Micah 7:8.

So, in the beginning: When the virgins were gathered together the second time, Mordecai was sitting at the king's gate Esther 2:19. But afterward: So Haman took the robes and the horse, and he arrayed Mordecai and made him ride through the open square of the city, proclaiming, Thus shall it be done to the man whom the king delights to honor Esther 6:11. And in the end: Then

Mordecai went out from the presence of the king in royal robes of blue and white, with a great golden crown and a mantle of fine linen and purple, while the city of Susa shouted and rejoiced Esther 8:15. And finally: The Jews had light and gladness and joy and honor Esther 8:16. —YERUSHALMI YOMA 3:2 III

This means that the issues of the law were drawn upward into the highest realm of Israelite consciousness. Keeping the law in the right way is represented as not merely right or expedient. It is the way to bring the Messiah, the son of David.

Said Rabbi Levi: If Israel would keep a single Sabbath in the proper way. forthwith the son of David would come. What is the scriptural basis for this view? Moses said: Eat it today, for today is a sabbath to the Lord; today you will not find it in the field Exodus 16:25. And it says: For thus said the Lord God, the Holy one of Israel: In returning and rest you shall be saved; in quietness and in trust shall be your strength. And you would not   Isaiah 30:15. —YERUSHALMI TAANIT 1:1 IX

The coming of the Messiah, moreover, was explicitly linked to the destruction of the Temple. How so? The Messiah was born on the day the Temple was destroyed. Accordingly, the consolation for the destruction of the Temple lay in the coming of the son of David.

The rabbis said: This messiah-king if he comes from among the living, David will be his name; if he comes from among the dead, it will be David himself. Said Rabbi Tanhuma: I say that the scriptural basis for this teaching is: And He shows steadfast love to His messiah, to David and his descendants forever Psalms 18:51.

Rabbi Joshua ben Levi said: "Sprout" [SeMaH] is his name. Rabbi Yudan, son of Rabbi Aibo, said: Menahem is his name. Said Hananiah, son of Rabbi Abbahu: They do not disagree. The numerical value of the letters of one name equals the numerical value of the other: SeMaH [=138] is equal to MeNaHeM [=138].

And this story supports the view of Rabbi Yudan, son of Rabbi Aibo: Once a Jew was plowing and his ox snorted once before him. An Arab who was passing and heard the sound said to him: Jew, loosen your ox and loosen the plow and stop plowing.

For today your Temple was destroyed. The ox snorted again. [The Arab] said to him: Jew, bind your ox and bind your plow. For today the messiah-king was born. [The Jew] said to him: What is his name? Menahem. He said to him: What is his father's name? [The Arab] said to him: Hezekiah. He said to him: Where is he from? He said to him: From the royal capital of Bethlehem in Judea.

He went and sold his ox and sold his plow. And he became a peddler of infants' felt-clothes. And he went from place to place until he came to that very city [Bethlehem]. All of the women bought from him. But Menahem's mother did not buy from him. He heard the women saying: Menahem's mother, Menahem's mother, come buy for your child. She said: I want to bring him up to hate Israel. For on the day he was born the Temple was destroyed. They said to her: We are sure that on this day it was destroyed and on this day it will be rebuilt.

She said to [the peddler]: I have no money. He said to her: It is no matter to me. Come and buy for him and pay me when I return. A while later he returned to that city. He said to her: How is the infant doing? She said to him: Since the time you saw him a wind came and carried him off away from me. —YERUSHALMI BERAKHOT 2:3 [Translated by Tzvee Zahavy]

REDEMPTION

On what account, then, will Israel be saved? The answer comes from the salvation from Egypt. The reasons that operated then still pertain now. First and most important, the time had come. It was God's choice, based upon God's and not Israel's wishes. God then responded to Israel's condition—the oppression, the outcry, the repentance. So there is a curious humanity to the transaction. God will do it in God's own time. But the condition of the people Israel helps God to decide the right time.

On account of five matters were the Israelites redeemed from Egypt: Because the end had come, because of oppression, because they cried out, because of the merit of the patriarchs, and because of repentance.

Because the end had come, as it is said: In the course of those many days the king of Egypt died. And the people of Israel groaned under their bondage, and cried out for help, and their cry under bondage came up to God. And God heard their groaning, and God remembered His covenant with Abraham, with Isaac, and with Jacob. And God saw the people of Israel, and God knew their condition Exodus 2:23-25.

Because of the oppression: And God heard their groaning.

Because they cried out: And God remembered His covenant.

Because of the merit of the patriarchs: And God remembered His covenant with Abraham, with Isaac, and with Jacob.

Because of penitence: And God knew their condition.

Because the end had come: And so Scripture says: When you are in tribulation, and all these things come upon you in the latter days, you will return to the Lord your God and obey His voice Deuteronomy 4:30.

You will return to the Lord — because of repentance.

For the Lord your God is a merciful God — because of mercy.

He will not fail you or destroy you or forget the covenant with your fathers Deuteronomy 4:31 — because of the merit of the patriarchs.

And so it says: Nevertheless He regarded their distress Psalms 106:44 — because of oppression.

When He heard their cry Psalms 106:44 — because of their outcry.

He remembered for their sake His covenant Psalms 106:45 — because of the merit of the patriarchs.

And relented according to the abundance of His steadfast love Psalms 106:45 — because of repentance.

And He caused them to be pitied Psalms 106:46 — because of mercy. —YERUSHALMI TAANIT 1:1 VII

IN THE MEANTIME
WHAT ARE WE TO DO?

In the meantime Israel must live the holy life of prayer, carrying out the commandments, studying the Torah, and attempting even to transcend the limits of God's requirements by doing acts of lovingkindness over and above the Torah's demands.

What sort of human being is shaped by the ideal of redemption and salvation at hand? Since Israel must submit and accept God's rule in order to be worthy of God's rule through God's anointed, so the individual must embody Israel's life. The individual must be submissive and accepting, neither hating nor causing hatred, in a state of perpetual repentance, struggling to break the power of the inclination to do evil. Jews should be people of unending goodwill and enduring acceptance of what is measured out to them. And, as we shall see in the next chapter, some of them were, and a number of them — sages in particular — acknowledged that, when they were not, then they had failed.

Rabbi Pedat in the name of Rabbi Jacob bar Idid: Rabbi Eleazar used to add after his prayer. What did he say? May it be Your will, Lord my God, God of my fathers, that no person come to hate us, nor that we come to hate any person, and that no person come to envy us, nor that we come to envy any person. And let Your Torah be our occupation all the days of our lives. And let our words be supplications before You.

The household of Rabbi Yannai say: When a person wakes up, he must say: Blessed are You Lord . . . who resurrects the dead. My Master I have sinned before You. May it be Your will, Lord my God, that You give to me a good heart, a good portion, a good inclination, a good associate, a good name, a good eye, and a good soul, and a humble soul and a modest spirit. And do not allow Your name to be profaned among us. And do not make us the subject of bad repute among Your creatures. And do not lead us in the end to destruction. And do not turn our hope to despair. And do not make our welfare dependent on other people. And do not make us depend for sustenance on others. For the beneficence of others is small, and their hatred may be great. And set our portion with Your

Torah, with those who do Your will. Rebuild Your house, Your courtyard, Your city, and Your Temple speedily in our days.

Rabbi Hiyya bar Abba prayed: May it be Your will, Lord our God, and God of our fathers, that You put in our hearts [the ability] fully to repent before You, so that our forefathers may not be put to shame in the world to come [on account of our sins].

Rabbi Tanhum bar Scholasticus prayed: And may it be Your will, Lord my God, God of my fathers, that You break the yoke of the inclination to do evil and remove it from our hearts. For You created us to do Your will. And we are obligated to do Your will as You desire. And we desire to do Your will. And what prevents us? That evil inclination which infects us. It is obvious to You that we do not have the strength to resist it. So let it be Your will, Lord my God, and God of my fathers, that You vanquish it from before us and subdue it, so that we may do Your will as our own will, with a whole heart.

Rabbi Yohanan used to pray: May it be Your will, Lord my God and God of my fathers, that You implant in our portion love and brotherhood, peace and friendship. And grant us a happy end and all our hopes. And fill our dominion with disciples. And grant that we may enjoy our portion of paradise. And provide for us a good heart and a good associate. And grant that we may rise early and find [each day] our hearts' desires. And let our souls' yearnings come before You for our future good. —YERUSHALMI BERAKHOT 4:2 II [Translated by Tzvee Zahavy]

5

Our Sages: Humanity "In Our Image, After Our Likeness"

THE READER OF THIS ANTHOLOGY of the Talmud of the Land of Israel should recognize by now that we are not dealing with wise sayings of a general nature. Nor are we surveying stories deriving from some unknown place and addressed to whom it may concern. The Yerushalmi speaks for a very distinctive group of people, expressing a particular viewpoint. The Talmud is the work of sages. It presents their well-crafted and remarkably unique view of things. In these pages, God has already spoken as a rabbi, out of rabbinic theology and law and within the idiom of rabbinic discourse. The ideals of humanity set forth to this point, the image of what a human being may become, derive not from Scripture alone but from Scripture joined to Mishnah and read as a single, integrated statement. So we turn from the world of humanity in general, of God and of Israel overall, to the images of the world of the sages in particular, to the portrait of men "like God" and of Israel "in Our image, after Our likeness." Who, then, is this rabbi, this new man?

Standing at this end of Bar Kokhba's war and looking backward, we discern in the entire antecedent history of Israel no holy man analagous to the rabbi. There were diverse sorts of holy men.

But the particular amalgam of definitive traits—charismatic clerk, savior-sage, lawyer-magician, and supernatural politician-bureaucrat—represented by the rabbi of this Talmud and the Babylonian one is not to be located in any former type of Israelite authority. Looking forward, from the formation of the Talmud onward, however, we rarely perceive a holy man wholly *unlike* the rabbi. None is out of touch with the rabbis' particular books. All present the knowledge of them as a source of legitimation, at least until we reach (for a brief moment) the earliest phase of Hassidism in the eighteenth century. From the two Talmuds onward, Jewish authorities carried weight because, whatever else they knew, they knew the Talmud and conformed to its laws and modes of thought. The heretic opposed the Talmud and violated its laws. So whoever exercised power did so because, whatever other basis for authority he may have enjoyed, he was made holy by knowledge of the writings of rabbis of this period.

THE HUMAN BEING "LIKE GOD"

If our sages think of the rabbi as "like God," it is because the rabbi conforms to the image of God revealed by God to Moses, who would be called "Our Rabbi" in the oral Torah taught exclusively by rabbis. It follows that at first our sages think of God in wholly anthropomorphic terms. To them, for humanity to be "like God" means that to begin with God is like humanity. They would not claim that the truly holy sage is God incarnate; that concept does not appear in the document at hand. But when they say, as they do, that God is the chief dancer among the righteous in the age to come, and that when a disciple greets his master, it is as if he greets God's "Presence" in the world, how far are we from the concept of God as model for man [and, in our own day, woman]?

Rabbi Berekhiah, Rabbi Helbo, Ulla Biria, Rabbi Eleazar in the name of Rabbi Hanina: In the future, the Holy One, blessed be He, is going to be the chief dancer among the righteous in the age to come. What is the scriptural basis for this view? Consider well her ramparts Psalms 48:14. It is written [and can be read as]: Her dance. And the righteous will point to Him with their finger [so saluting Him], and say: That this is God, our God for ever and ever. He will be our guide for ever Psalms 48:15. —YERUSHALMI MOED QATAN 3:7 XI

Rabbi Berekhiah, Rabbi Jeremiah in the name of Rabbi Hiyya bar Ba: It is written: Now Moses used to take the tent [and pitch it outside the camp, far off from the camp; and he called it the tent of meeting. And every one who sought the Lord would go out to the tent of meeting, which was outside the camp] Exodus 33:7.

And how far was it? Rabbi Isaac said: A *mil*.

And everyone who sought Moses is not written here. Rather what is written is: And every one who sought the Lord. This indicates that whoever greets his master is as if he greets the indwelling Presence.

Rabbi Helbo, Rabbi Huna in the name of Rab: It is written: Now Elijah, the Tishbite, of Tishbe in Gilead, said to Ahab: As the Lord the God of Israel lives, before whom I stand. . . . 1 Kings 17:1. Now [at this point] was Elijah not merely an apprentice to the prophets? [How could he speak as a prophet, saying, before whom I stand?] But this teaches that every time he stood before Ahijah, the Shilonite, his master, it was as if he stood before the indwelling Presence.

Rabbi Helbo in the name of members of the household of Shiloh: Even if Elijah asked for water before him, Elisha would pour it on his hands. What is the scriptural basis for this statement? [And Jehoshaphat said: Is there no prophet of the Lord here, through whom we may inquire of the Lord? Then one of the king of Israel's servants answered:] Elisha the son of Shaphat is here, who poured water on the hands of Elijah 2 Kings 3:11. It is not written: . . . who studied Torah . . ., but rather, who poured water on the hands of Elijah.

It is written: Now the boy Samuel was ministering to the Lord under Eli. And the word of the Lord was rare in those days; there was no frequent vision 1 Samuel 3:1. But is it not the case that he was ministering only to Eli [and not directly to the Lord]? This indicates that every act of service he performed before Eli, his master, is as if he performed it before the indwelling Presence.

Rabbi Ishmael taught: [And Jethro, Moses' father-in-law, offered a burnt offering and sacrifices to God;] and Aaron came with all the elders of Israel to eat bread with Moses' father-in-law before God Exodus 18:12. Now was it before God that they were eating? Rather, this teaches that he who receives his fellow is as if he receives the indwelling Presence. —YERUSHALMI ERUBIN 5:1 III

Along these same lines, we find stories about gentile authorities who pay respect to sages because in their faces they see angels.

Rabbi Yohanan was sitting and reciting before a congregation of Babylonians in Sepphoris. An official passed by, but Yohanan did not stand before him. The [official's guard] went to strike him. He said to them: Leave him be! He is absorbed in his Creator's laws.

Rabbi Hanina and Rabbi Joshua ben Levi went before the proconsul of Caesarea. When he saw them he stood up. [His courtiers] said to him: Why do you stand up for these Jews? He said to them: I see in them the faces of angels.

Rabbi Jonah and Rabbi Yose went before Ursicinus, governor of Antioch. When he saw them he stood up. They said to him: Why do you stand up for these Jews? He said to them: I saw their faces in a vision during a battle and I was victorious. —YERUSHALMI BERAKHOT 5:1 [Translated by Tzvee Zahavy]

THE SAGE "LIKE GOD"

What makes the sage "like God" is not solely mastery of divine revelation but, especially, true moral distinction. This message is framed, to begin with, in stories about outsiders — Jews who were not sages, but who were supernaturally recognized for their remarkable moral character. The message of these stories is that one need not be a sage to be "like God."

A certain man came before one of the relatives of Rabbi Yannai. He said to him: Rabbi, attain merit through me [by giving charity]. He said to him: And didn't your father leave you money? He said to him: No. He said to him: Go and collect what your father left on deposit with others. He said to him: I have heard concerning property my father deposited with others that it was gained by violence [so I do not want it]. He said to him: You are worthy of having your prayers answered.

A certain ass-driver appeared before the rabbis [in a dream] and prayed, and rain came. [Realizing he was a holy man,] the rabbis sent for him and said to him: What is your trade? He said to them: I am an ass-driver. They said to him: And how do you conduct your business? He said to them: One time I rented my ass to a certain woman, and she was weeping on the way, and I said to her: What's the matter with you? And she said to me: The husband of this woman [referring to herself] is in prison [for debt], and I wanted to see what I can do to free him.

So I sold my ass and I gave her the proceeds, and I said to her: Here is your money, free your husband, but do not sin [by becoming a prostitute to raise the necessary funds].

They said to him: You are worthy of praying and having your prayers answered.

In a dream Mr. Pentakaka ["Five Sins"] appeared to Rabbi Abbahu, who prayed that rain would come, and it rained. Rabbi Abbahu summoned him. He said to him: What is your trade? He said to him: Five sins does that man [referring to himself] do every day—hiring whores, cleaning up the theater, bringing home their garments for washing, dancing, and performing before them.

He said to him: And what sort of decent thing have you ever done? He said to him: One day that man [I] was cleaning the theater, and a woman came and stood behind a pillar and cried. I said to her: What's the matter with you? And she said to me: This woman's [referring to herself] husband is in prison, and I wanted to see what I can do to free him.

So I sold my bed and cover, and I gave the proceeds to her. I said to her: Here is your money, free your husband, but do not sin.

He said to him: You are worthy of praying and having your prayers answered.

A pious man from Kefar Imi appeared [in a dream] to the rabbis. He prayed for rain and it rained. The rabbis went up to him. His householders told them that he was sitting on a hill. They went out to him, saying to him: Greetings. But he did not answer them. He was sitting and eating, and he did not say to them: You break bread, too.

When he went back home, he made a bundle of faggots and put his cloak on top of the bundle [instead of on his shoulder]. When he came home, he said to his [wife]: These rabbis are here [because] they want me to pray for rain. If I pray and it rains, it is a disgrace for them, and if not, it is a profanation of the Name of Heaven. But come, you and I will go up [to the roof] and pray. If it rains, we shall tell them: Heaven has wrought a miracle [for you]. And if not, we shall tell them: We are not worthy to pray and have our prayers answered.

They went up and prayed, and it rained. They came down to them [and asked]: Why have the rabbis troubled themselves to come here today? They said to him: We wanted you to pray so that it would rain. He said to them: Now do you really need my prayers? Heaven has already done its miracle.

They said to him: Why, when you were on the hill and we said hello to you, did you not reply? He said to them: It was then doing my job. Should I then interrupt my concentration [on my work]?

They said to him: And why, when you sat down to eat, did you not say to us: You break bread, too? He said to them: Because I had only my small ration of bread. Why should I have invited you to eat by way of mere flattery [when I knew I could not give you anything at all]?

They said to him: And why, when you came to go down, did you put your cloak on top of the bundle? He said to them: Because the cloak was not mine. It was borrowed for use at prayer. I did not want to tear it.

They said to him: And why, when you were on the hill, did your wife wear dirty clothes, but when you came down from the mountain, she put on clean clothes? He said to them: When I was on the hill, she put on dirty clothes, so that no one would gaze at her. But when I came home from the hill, she put on clean clothes, so that I would not gaze at any other woman. —YERUSHALMI TAANIT 1:4 I

There is the story of a certain pious man, who went to take a stroll in his vineyard on the Sabbath. He saw a hole in a wall and thought of fencing it up at the end of the Sabbath. He then said: Since on the Sabbath I gave thought to fencing it up after the Sabbath, lo, I shall never fence it up.

What did the Holy One, blessed be He, do for him? He arranged for a booth consisting of a caperbush to grow up there, and it grew and filled in the fence. The man derived sustenance from the caperbush and gained benefit from it his entire life. – YERUSHALMI SHABBAT 15:3 I

The image of humanity, as portrayed above, conforms to the image of God when humanity acts like God and so exhibits exemplary virtues, to which God responds. Ordinary folk may be in God's image, yet the bulk of tales of profound moral insight pertain, not surprisingly, to sages themselves, not common people. These focus upon sages' capacity to accept suffering and to submit to the punishment that leads to regeneration.

Nahum of Gim Zu was bringing a gift to the household of his father-in-law. A person afflicted with boils met him and said to him: Acquire merit with me by giving me part of what you have in hand. He said to him: Wait till I come back. But when he got back, he found the man dead.

He said: Let the eyes that saw you and did not receive you be plucked out. Let the hands that did not reach out and give to you be cut off. Let the legs that did not run to give something to you be broken.

And so it happened to him.

Rabbi Aqiba said to him: Woe is me, that I see you in such a condition! [Nahum] said to him: Woe is me, that I do not see you in such a condition!

He said to him: Why do you curse me? [Nahum] said to him: Why do you rebel against suffering? —YERUSHALMI SHEQALIM 5:4 I

Rabbi Aqiba was on trial before Tonosteropos, the wicked. The time for reciting the *Shema* came. He began to recite it and smiled. [The wicked one] said to him: Old man, old man! You are either a wizard or you have contempt for pain [that you smile].

[As if taking an oath, Aqiba] said to him: May the soul of this man [referring to himself] perish. I am no wizard, nor do I have contempt for pain. But for my whole life I have been reciting this verse: And you shall love the Lord your God with all your heart, with all your soul, and with all your might Deuteronomy 6:5. Now I loved God with all my heart, and I loved Him with all my might. But with all my soul until now was not demanded of me. And now that the time has come for me to love Him with all my soul, as the time for reciting *Shema* has arrived, I smile that the occasion has come to carry out the verse at that very moment at which I recite the Scripture. —YERUSHALMI SOTAH 5:5 IV

In these ways, as we have seen, the sage in his own life embodies the situation of Israel, doing those very deeds that in the end will save the nation. Through unusual humility, exemplary honesty, and applied and practiced wisdom, sages show here and now what it means to be "like God."

Rabbi Zabedah, son-in-law of Rabbi Levi, would tell the following story.

Rabbi Meir would teach a lesson in the synagogue of Hammata every Sabbath night. There was a woman who would come regularly to hear him. One time the lesson lasted longer than usual. She went home and found that the light had gone out. Her husband said to her: Where have you been? She replied to him: I was listening to the lesson. He said to her: May God do such-and-so and even more, if this woman enters my house before she goes and spits in the face of that sage who gave the lesson.

Rabbi Meir perceived with the help of the Holy Spirit [what had happened] and he pretended to have a pain in his eye. He said: Any woman who knows how to recite a charm over an eye—let her come and heal mine.

The woman's neighbors said to her: Lo, your time to go back home has come. Pretend to be a charmer and go and spit in Rabbi Meir's eye.

She came to him. He said to her: Do you know how to heal a sore eye through making a charm? She became frightened and said to him: No. He said to her: Do they not spit into it seven times, and is it not good for it?

After she had spit in his eye, he said to her: Go and tell your husband that you did it one time. She said to him: And lo, I spit seven times?

Rabbi Meir's disciples said to him: Rabbi, in such a way do they disgracefully treat the Torah [which is yours]? If you had told us about the incident with the husband, would we not have brought him and flogged him at the stock, until he was reconciled with his wife?

He said to them: And should the honor owing to Meir be tantamount to the honor owing to Meir's creator? Now if Scripture has said the Holy Name, which is written in a state of sanctification, is to be blotted out with water so as to bring peace between a man and his wife, should not the honor owing to Meir be dealt with in the same way! —YERUSHALMI SOTAH 1:4 II

Rabbi Jonathan was an exemplary judge. He had as a neighbor an Aramean [pagan], who lived next door in the field and in the village. Now Rabbi Jonathan had a tree planted [so that it overshadowed the property] of the Aramean. A case along the lines [of the situation prevailing for Jonathan and his Aramean neighbor] came before [Jonathan]. He said to them: Go and come back tomorrow.

Now the Aramean thought to himself: It is on my account that he made no ruling. Tomorrow I shall go and chop off the branches which overshadow my property on my own, and I shall see how he decides the other case. If he judges other people but does not apply the judgment to himself, he is not a decent person.

At evening Rabbi Jonathan sent instructions to his carpenter, saying: Go, cut off the part of the tree which is overshadowing the Aramean's land.

In the morning, the litigant came before Rabbi Jonathan. He said to him: Go, cut the branches which are overhanging your land.

The Aramean then said to him: And what is the law concerning your branches? He said to him: Go and see how my branches are treated in your property [for they already had been cut off].

[The Aramean] went out and saw the pruning which had taken place, and he said: Blessed be the God of the Jews.

A certain woman [having a case before Jonathan] brought him a present of figs. He said to her: By your leave, if you brought them in uncovered, take them out uncovered, and if you brought them in covered up, take them out covered up, so that people won't say that you brought in money, when in fact you brought a gift of figs [which in any case I shall not accept].

Rabbi Hanina came to visit Rabbi Jonathan in his garden and [Jonathan] brought him figs to eat. When he went out, he saw that [elsewhere in the garden] he had white Bath Sheba figs [that is, figs of a far higher quality]. He said to him: Now why did you not feed me some of these [which are of better quality]? He said to him: They are my son's. Rabbi Hanina scrupled about not taking them without permission from the son, and so committing an act of theft against him. —YERUSHALMI BABA BATRA 2:13 I

Rabbi Samuel bar Suseretai went to Rome. The queen had lost her jewelry. He found it. A proclamation went forth through the city: Whoever returns her jewelry in thirty days will receive thus-and-so. [If he returns it] after thirty days, his head will be cut off.

He did not return the jewelry within thirty days. After thirty days, he returned it to her. She said to him: Weren't you in town? He said to her: Yes [I was here].

She said to him: And didn't you hear the proclamation? He said to her: Yes [I heard it]. She said to him: And what did it say? He said to her: It said: Whoever returns her jewelry in thirty days will receive thus-and-so. [If he returns it] after thirty days, his head will be cut off.

She said to him: And why didn't you return it within thirty days? [Samuel replied:] So that people should not say: It was because I was afraid of you that I did so. But it was because I fear the All-Merciful.

She said to him: Blessed be the God of the Jews.

Alexander of Macedon went to the king of Qasya [who resides behind the Dark Mountain]. He showed him that he had a great deal of gold and silver. [Alexander] said to him: I don't need your gold and your silver. I came only to see your customs, how you distribute [alms], how you judge [cases].

While he was chatting with him, someone came with a case against his fellow. He had bought a piece of a field with its rubbish dump, and he had found a trove of money in it. The one who had bought the property said: I bought a junk pile; I did not buy a trove. The one who had sold the property said: A junk pile and everything in it is what I sold you.

While they were arguing with one another, the king said to one of them: Do you have a male child? He said to him: Yes. [The king] said to his fellow: Do you have a female child? He said to him: Yes.

He said to them: Let this one marry that one, and let the treasure-trove belong to the two of them.

[Alexander] began to laugh. He said to him: Now why are you laughing? Didn't I judge the case properly?

He said to him: If such a case came before you, how would you have judged it? [Alexander] said to him: We should have killed both this one and that one, and kept the treasure for the king. He said to him: Do you people love gold all that much?

He made a banquet for [Alexander] and laid out before him gold loaves and gold chickens. [Alexander] said to him: Can I eat the gold?

[The king] said to him: May this man's [referring to himself] soul be struck down. You don't eat gold? Then why do you love it so much?

[The king of Qasya, a gentile ruler,] said to him: Does the sun shine in your land? [Alexander] said to him: Yes.

Does it rain in your land? [Alexander] said to him: Yes.

He said to him: In your town is there some sort of small beast? [Alexander] said to him: Yes.

Then may the soul of this man be smitten! You live only by the merit of that small beast, since it is written: **Man and beast do you save O Lord** Psalms 36:7. —YERUSHALMI BABA MESIA 2:5 I

THE SAGE, NOT LIKE OTHER MEN

The example of rabbinical virtue was adduced explicitly to account for the supernatural or magical power of a rabbi. He afforded protection, through his learning of Torah from this-worldly and supernatural enemies.

Rabbi Yudan the Patriarch sent Rabbi Hiyya, Rabbi Asi, and Rabbi Ami to travel among the towns of the Land of Israel to provide for them scribes and teachers. They came to one place and found neither scribe nor teacher. They said to the people: Bring us the guardians of the town.

The people brought them the citizens of senatorial class in that town. [The rabbis] said to them: Do you think these are the guardians of the town? They are none other than the destroyers of the town.

They said to them: And who are the guardians of the town?
They said to them: The scribes and teachers.

That is in line with what is written: Unless the Lord builds
the house, those who build it labor in vain. Unless the Lord
watches over the city, the watchman stays awake in vain Psalms 127:1.
—YERUSHALMI HAGIGAH 1:7 II

Rabbi Jacob bar Idi and Rabbi Isaac bar Nahman were super-
visors [of the communal funds]. They would give Rabbi Hama,
father of Rabbi Hoshaia, a *denar*. He then would divide it among
others [who needed it].

Rabbi Zechariah, father-in-law of Rabbi Levi, was subject
to public scandal. People said that he was not in need but he took
[charity anyhow]. After he died, they looked into the matter and
found that he would divide up [the funds] among others [in need].

Rabbi Hinena bar Papa would pass out charity funds by
night. One time the lord of the spirits met him. He said to him: Did
not Our Rabbi [Moses] teach us: You shall not remove your neighbor's landmark Deuteronomy 19:14 [meaning, you should not be out at
night, over which I rule]. [Hinena] said to him: Is it not written:
A gift in secret averts anger; and a bribe in the bosom, strong
wrath Proverbs 21:14? The other stepped back from him and fled.

Said Rabbi Jonah: Happy is he who gives to the poor is not
written here, but rather: Blessed is he who considers the poor
Psalms 41:2. This refers to one who examines the religious duty of
charity, figuring out how to do it properly.

How then did Rabbi Jonah do it? When he saw a poor person,
son of worthy parents, who had lost his property, he would say to
him: Since I heard that you have inherited property from some
other source, take some money now and pay me back later on.

When the poor person would take the money, he would say
to him: It is a gift for you. —YERUSHALMI SHEQALIM 5:4 I

*There was no doubt, in people's imagination, that the reason
the rabbis could do the amazing things people said they did was
that they embodied the law and exercised its supernatural or magical power.*

There was a house that was about to collapse over there [in
Babylonia], and Rab sent one of his disciples into the house, until

they had cleared everything out from the house. When the disciple left the house, the house collapsed. And there are those who say that it was Rabbi Adda bar Ahwah.

Sages sent and said to him: What sort of good deeds are to your credit [that you have that much merit]? He said to them: In my whole life no man ever got to the synagogue in the morning before I did. I never left anybody there when I went out. I never walked four cubits without speaking words of Torah. Nor did I ever mention teachings of Torah in an inappropriate setting. I never laid out a bed and slept for a regular period of time. I never took great strides among the associates. I never called my fellow by a nickname. I never rejoiced in the embarrassment of my fellow. I never cursed my fellow when I was lying by myself in bed. I never walked over in the marketplace to someone who owed me money. In my entire life I never lost my temper in my household.

This was meant to carry out that which is stated as follows: I will give heed to the way that is blameless. Oh when will You come to me? I will walk with integrity of heart within my house Psalms 101:2. —YERUSHALMI TAANIT 3:11 IV

Rabbi Yosa fasted eighty fasts in order to see Rabbi Hiyya the Elder [in a dream]. He finally saw him, and his hands trembled and his eyes grew dim. Now if you say that Rabbi Yosa was an unimportant man, [and so was unworthy of such a vision, that is not the case]. For a weaver came before Rabbi Yohanan. He said to him: I saw in my dream that the Heaven fell, and one of your disciples was holding it up. He said to him: Will you know him [when you see him]? He said to him: When I see him, I shall know him.

Then all of his disciples passed before [the weaver], and he recognized Rabbi Yosa. —YERUSHALMI KETUBOT 12:3 VII

There was a case in which a fire broke out in the courtyard of Yose ben Simai in Shihin, and the Roman soldiers of the camp of Sepphoris came down to put it out. But [Yose] did not let them do so. [He did not want the gentiles to work for him on the Sabbath.] He said to them: Let the Tax-Collector come and collect what is owing to him.

Forthwith clouds gathered, and rain came and put the fire out. After the Sabbath he sent a *sela* to every soldier, and to their commander he sent fifty *denars.* Said Rabbi Hanina: It was not necessary to do so [but he rewarded them, so that they would help out in the future]. —YERUSHALMI NEDARIM 4:9 I

The correlation between learning and teaching, on the one side, and supernatural power or recognition, on the other, is explicit.

When Rabbi Eleazar, Rabbi Joshua, and Rabbi Aqiba went in to bathe in the baths of Tiberias, a *min* (heretic) saw them. He said what he said, and the arched chamber in the bath [where idolatrous statues were put up] held them fast [so that they could not move].

Said Rabbi Eleazar to Rabbi Joshua: Now Joshua ben Hanina, see what you can do.

When that *min* tried to leave, Rabbi Joshua said what he said, and the doorway of the bath seized and held the *min* firm, so that whoever went in had to give him a knock [to push by], and whoever went out had to give him a knock [to push by]. [The *min*] said to them: Undo whatever you have done [and let me go]. They said to him: Release us, and we shall release you. They released one another.

Once they got outside, Rabbi Joshua said to that *min*: Lo, is that all you know? He [replied], Let's go down to the sea.

When they got down to the sea, that *min* said whatever it was that he said, and the sea split open. He said to them: Now is this not what Moses, your rabbi, did at the sea?

They said to him: Do you not concede to us that Moses, Our Rabbi, walked through it? He said to them: Yes. They said to him: Then walk through it.

He walked through it. Rabbi Joshua [through sorcery] instructed the ruler of the sea, who swallowed him up.

When Rabbi Eliezer, Rabbi Joshua, and Rabban Gamaliel went up to Rome, they came to a certain place and found children making little piles [of dirt]. They said: Children of the Land of Israel make this sort of thing, and they say: This is heave offering, and [they say:] That is tithe. It's likely that Jews are here.

They came into one place and were received there. When they sat down to eat, [they noticed that] each dish which they brought in to them would first be taken into a small room, and then brought to them, and they wondered whether they might be eating sacrifices offered to the dead. [That is, they suspected that in the small chamber a sacrificial portion was removed from each dish and offered to an idol.]

They said to [their host]: What is your purpose: as to every dish which you bring before us, if you do not take it first into a small room, you do not bring it in to us?

He said to them: I have a very old father, and he has made a decree for himself that he will never go out of that small room until he sees the sages of Israel. They said to him: Go and tell him: Come out here to them, for they are here.

He came out to them. They said to him: Why do you do this? He said to them: Pray for my son, for he has not produced a child.

Said Rabbi Eliezer to Rabbi Joshua: Now, Joshua ben Hananiah, let us see what you will do.

[Joshua] said to them: Bring me flax seeds. And they brought him flax seeds. He appeared to sow the seed on the table; he appeared to scatter the seed; he appeared to bring the seed up; he appeared to take hold of it, until he drew up a woman, holding on to her tresses.

He said to her: Release whatever [magic] you have done [to this man]. She said to him: I am not going to release [my spell]. He said to her: If you don't do it, I shall publicize your [magical secrets]. She said to him: I cannot do it, for [the magical materials] have been cast into the sea.

Rabbi Joshua made a decree that the sea release [the magical materials], and they came up. They prayed for [the host], and he had the merit of producing a son, Rabbi Judah ben Bathera.

They said: If we came up here only for the purpose of producing that righteous man, it would have been enough for us.

Said Rabbi Joshua ben Hananiah: I can take cucumbers and pumpkins and turn them into rams and hosts of rams, and they will produce still more.

Said Rabbi Yannai: I was going along in the road in Sepphoris, and I saw a *min*, who took a pebble and threw it up into the sky, and it came down and was turned into a calf.

And did not Rabbi Eleazar say in the name of Rabbi Yose bar Zimra: If everyone in the world got together, they could not create a single mosquito and put breath into it? But we must say that the *min* did not take a pebble and throw it up into the air, so when it came down it was turned into a calf. But he ordered his servant to steal a calf from the herd and bring it to him.

Said Rabbi Hinena ben Rabbi Hananiah: I was walking in the turf[?] of Sepphoris, and I saw a *min* take a skull and throw it up into the air, and when it came down, it had turned into a calf. And I came and told father, and he said to me: If you actually ate of the calf-meat, it really happened, and if not, it was a mere illusion. — YERUSHALMI SANHEDRIN 7:13 III

6

Our Sages:
Humanity at
Its Most Human

THE TALMUD OF THE LAND OF ISRAEL depicts the sage not only "like God" but also under the aspect of humanity. The sage is deeply human and represented as much like, and sometimes worse than other people. The sage pays meticulous attention to matters of precedence and standing. While rationalized as an issue of respect for the Torah, the obsession is not so represented under all circumstances. The sage grows angry, engages in venomous vendettas against other sages, enforces his will by all means at his disposal, and, in general, acts like any other intellectual in his day (or ours). The fact that the Talmud portrays the sage as wholly human, as well as in some ways God-like, emphasizes the frail and mortal character of the Talmud's images of humanity. That is all the more reason, then, to celebrate the possibility of humanity's becoming God-like through the Torah.

THE SAGE,
LIKE THE REST OF US

The sages depicted by the Talmud carefully weighed every detail of personal honor and prestige. Issues over which they might fight bitterly appear intangible, but, involving as they did matters of self-esteem and standing, provoked fierce contention. In their context, these stories illustrate values the storytellers may well have considered noble. But in our view, their humanity hardly differs from our own. Perhaps the issues were trivial because weak, poor people found meaning wherever they might. But, as we shall now see, not only greatness but smallness and pettiness characterize sages' relationships among themselves and with the world at large. In turn, this rather sizable repertoire of stories concern petty slights, pursuing one's privileges, jealousy, ingratitude or niggardliness (depending upon perspective), meddling, a long-standing vendetta over petty slights between great sages, and out-and-out cowardice.

Rabbi would make two appointments [to his administration, at one time]. If they proved worthy, [the appointees] were confirmed. If not, they were removed.

When he was dying, he instructed his son [Gamaliel]: Don't do it that way. Rather appoint them all at one time.

[Gamaliel] appointed Rabbi Hami bar Hanina at the head [of the group]. And why had Rabbi not appointed him? It was because the people of Sepphoris were opposed to him. And merely because people raise a cry, do [sages] do the things they want? [Obviously not!] Said Rabbi Eleazar ben Rabbi Yose: It was because [Hami ben Hanina] publicly contradicted [what Rabbi said].

[This is the story.] Rabbi was in session. He cited the following verse: Then those of you who escape will remember Me among the nations where they are carried captive, when I have broken their wanton heart which has departed from Me, and blinded their eyes which turn wantonly after their idols; and they will be loathsome in their own sight for the evils which they have committed, for all their abominations Ezekiel 6:9. And if any survivors escape, they will be on the mountains, like doves of the valleys, all of them moaning, every one over his iniquity Ezekiel 7:16.

[Hami ben Hanina] said to him: We read the verse as, *roar.* [Rabbi] said to him: Where did you study Scripture? He said to him: Before Rabbi Hamnuna of Babylonia. [Rabbi] said to him: When you go down there, tell him to appoint you a sage.

[Hami ben Hanina] realized that he would not be appointed [a sage in Rabbi's administration] for the rest of his life. – YERUSHALMI TAANIT 4:2

The teacher of the son of Rabbi Hoshaia the Elder was blind, and he was accustomed to eat with him every day. One day he had guests, and he did not come to eat with [his teacher] in the evening. He came to him, saying to him: May my master not be angry with me, for I had guests today, and I thought that I would not allow my master's honor to be cheapened today, so I did not eat with my master today.

[His teacher] said to him: You have thereby appeased one who is seen but does not see. May the One who sees but is not seen accept your excuse.

He said to him: Whence did you learn this [curse]?

[His teacher] said to him: From Rabbi Eliezer ben Jacob. For to the town of Rabbi Eliezer ben Jacob a blind man came. Rabbi Eliezer ben Jacob sat below him, so that people would say: If it were not that this man was a great man, Rabbi Eliezer ben Jacob would not have seated himself lower than he. They paid the blind man great honor [and supplied his needs]. The blind man asked: Why thus? They said to him, Rabbi Eliezer ben Jacob sat below you.

So the blind man prayed this prayer: You have acted faithfully with one who is seen but does not see. May He who sees but is not seen act faithfully with you. —YERUSHALMI SHEQALIM 5:4 I

Rabbi began to pay respect to Hiyya. When he would come into the meeting house, he would say: Let Hiyya the Elder go in before me.

Rabbi Ishmael ben Rabbi Yose said to [Rabbi]: Even before me? He said to him: Heaven forfend! Rabbi Hiyya the Elder may be within, but Rabbi Ishmael ben Rabbi Yose is innermost.

Rabbi was praising Rabbi Hiyya the Elder in the presence of Rabbi Ishmael ben Yose. One time he saw him in the bathhouse and

[Hiyya] did not rise to pay his respects to [Ishmael]. Ishmael said to [Rabbi]: Is this the one whom you were praising to me?

He said to him: What did he do to you? [Ishmael] said to him: I saw him in the bathhouse, and he did not rise to pay his respects to me.

He said to [Hiyya]: Why did you behave in such a way? He said to him: May a terrible thing happen to me, if I even noticed him. I knew nothing about it. At the time I was reviewing the aggadic traditions of the whole Book of Psalms. —YERUSHALMI KETUBOT 12:3 VI

[As to Mishnah Megillah 1:4, giving gifts:] Rabbi Yudan the Patriarch sent to Rabbi Hoshaia a piece of meat and a flask of wine. He replied, saying to him: In us have you carried out the following verse of Scripture: [As the days on which the Jews got relief from their enemies, and as the month that had been turned for them from sorrow into gladness and from mourning into a holiday; that they should make them days of feasting and gladness, days for sending choice portions to one another and] gifts to the poor Esther 9:22.

He went and sent him a calf and a barrel of wine. He sent back to him: Through us you have carried out the following verse of Scripture: [As the days on which the Jews got relief from their enemies, and as the month that had been turned for them from sorrow into gladness and from mourning into a holiday; that they should make them days of feasting and gladness, days for] sending choice portions to one another [and gifts to the poor]. —YERUSHALMI MEGILLAH 1:4 XI

Rabbi was marrying off Rabbi Simeon, his son, and on that occasion on the Sabbath the people were clapping by striking together the backs of their hands. Rabbi Meir happened by and heard the noise. He said: Have our rabbis [Rabbi] declared [this kind of clapping] permitted on the Sabbath?

Rabbi heard about it and said: Who is this who had come to persecute us in our own house? And there is one who says: Who is this one who has come to belittle us in our own home?

Rabbi Meir heard about it and fled. The youngsters [participants in the wedding] went out after him. The wind picked up

[Meir's] turban from around his neck. Rabbi looked out of the window and saw Meir's [naked] neck from the back. He said: I have had the merit of learning Torah only because I saw Rabbi Meir's naked neck from the back. —YERUSHALMI BESAH 5:2 VI

Rabbi Yohanan was leaning on Rabbi Jacob bar Iddi, and Rabbi Eleazar [a Babylonian] saw him and avoided him. [Yohanan] said: Lo, now there are two things that that Babylonian has done to me! One is that he didn't even bother to greet me, and the other is that he didn't cite a tradition of mine in my name.

[Jacob] said to him: That is the custom over there, that the lesser party does not greet the more important authority. For they carry out the following verse of Scripture: The young men saw me and withdrew, and the aged rose and stood Job 29:8.

As they were going along, they saw a certain schoolhouse. [Jacob] said to him: Here is where Rabbi Meir used to go into session and expound the law. And he stated traditions in the name of Rabbi Aqiba. [Yohanan] said to him: Everybody knows that Rabbi Meir was the disciple of Rabbi Aqiba [so he did not have to cite him]. [Jacob] said to him: Everybody knows that Rabbi Eleazar is the disciple of Rabbi Yohanan.

As they were going along, [they passed by a procession in which an idol was carried, and Jacob asked Yohanan:] What is the law as to passing a procession in which an idol is being carried? He said to him: And do you pay respect to the idol. Go before it and blind its eyes. [Jacob] said to him: Well did Rabbi Eleazar do to you, for he did not pass by you [since that would have required an inappropriate gesture].

[Yohanan] said to him: Jacob bar Iddi, you know well how to make peace [between quarreling people].

Rabbi Yohanan wanted traditions to be stated in his name, for David too prayed for mercy [for the same purpose], saying: Let me dwell in Your tent for ever! Oh to be safe under the shelter of Your wings! Psalms 61:5. —YERUSHALMI MOED QATAN 3:7 XIX

Rabbi Dosetai ben Rabbi Yannai and Rabbi Yose ben Kefar went down [to Babylonia] to collect money over there for the associates. [After they collected money,] people spoke ill of them, saying they did not want to give them a thing. The donors came and demanded the money back. They said to [the donors]: We already have acquired possession of it.

[The donors] said to them: We want you to undertake a careful [charge of the money, and make it up if it is lost]. They said to them: We are gratuitous bailees [and are not obliged to make it up if it is lost].

They sent to Rabbi Dosetai ben Yanni. He said to them: Here it all is.

They took Rabbi Yose ben Kefar and tied him up and took it away from him.

When they came up here [returned to the Land of Israel, Dosetai] came before his father and said to him: See what your son has done to me! He said to him: What did he do to you?

[Dosetai] said to him: If [Yose] had agreed with me, they would not have taken a thing from us. [His father] said to him: Why did you do so? [Why did you merely hand over the money when the donors demanded it?]

[Dosetai] said to him: I saw that they were a completely unanimous court [of judges], and their Adam's apples were a cubit high, and they speak from their bellies, and my brother Yose was tied up, and the strap was rising and falling on him, and I said to myself: Is it possible that father has another Dosetai besides me at home? —YERUSHALMI QIDDUSHIN 3:4 II

... OR WORSE

The sages exhibited not only commonplace failings but also egregious ones. They had to be warned against turning their religious virtues into out-and-out vices. The Talmud tells us, for example, how idiots might, in the name of piety, allow people to drown, and how in the cause of religious observance they might turn the holy way of life into a system of trivial brokerage, trading benefit for service.

What is meant by "a foolish saint" [referring to Mishnah Sotah 3:4: **A foolish saint wears out the world**.]?

If one saw a child drowning in a river and said: When I have removed my phylacteries, I shall save him . . . [and] while this one was removing his phylacteries, the other gave up the ghost—

If he found a fig which was the first of the season, and said:
Whomever I shall meet first, I shall give it to him [so as not to benefit from first-fruits], if he then saw a betrothed maiden and ran
after her [for that purpose] —

This is in line with that which we have taught: **He who runs
after his fellow to kill him, after a male, after a betrothed
maiden....** Mishnah Sanhedrin 8:7

[What does Mishnah mean by] **a smart knave** Mishnah Sotah
3:4? Rabbi Zeriqan in the name of Rabbi Huna: This is one who
applies lenient rulings to himself and strict rulings to other people.

[What does Mishnah mean by] **an abstemious woman** Mishnah Sotah 3:4? This is one who sits and quotes biblical phrases in a
suggestive way: And she said: You must come into me, for I have
hired you with my son's mandrakes; and he lay with her that night
Genesis 30:16.

[What does Mishnah mean by] **blows of abstainers** Mishnah
Sotah 3:4? This is the sort of person who gives advice to heirs of an
estate on how to keep the widow from getting her rightful maintenance. —YERUSHALMI SOTAH 3:4 VIII-XI

*The great disciplines of sanctification might thus generate
hypocrisy.*

There are seven types of Pharisees: the shoulder-Pharisee;
the wait-a-while Pharisee; the book-keeping Pharisee; the niggardly Pharisee; the show-me-what-I-did-wrong Pharisee; the
Pharisee out of fear; and the Pharisee out of love.

"The shoulder-Pharisee" carries the religious deeds he has
done on his shoulder [for all to see].

"The wait-a-while Pharisee"–Wait a minute, while I go off
and do a religious deed.

"The book-keeping Pharisee"– He does one deed for which
he is liable and one deed which is a religious duty, and then he
balances one off against the other.

"The niggardly Pharisee"–Who will show me how to save,
so that I can do a religious deed?

"The show-me-what-I-did-wrong Pharisee"– Show me what
sin I have done, and I will do an equivalent religious duty.

"A Pharisee out of fear"– like Job.

"A Pharisee out of love"– like Abraham.

And the only one of them all who is truly beloved is the Pharisee out of love, like Abraham. —YERUSHALMI SOTAH 5:5 II

A rabbi could not be trusted to protect the trade secrets of his benefactor. The story below is told by two storytellers and the evaluation of Yohanan's failure to keep his word is unclear. One storyteller seems to approve while the other does not.

Rabbi Yohanan had [scurvy], and he was receiving treatment from [the daughter of] Domitian in Tiberias. On Friday he went to her. He said to her: Do I need to be treated tomorrow [on the Sabbath]?

She said to him: No. But if you should need something, put on seeds of date palms (and some say: seeds of Nicolaos dates), split in half and roasted, and pounded together with barley husks and a child's dried excrement, and apply that mixture. But do not reveal to anyone [this potion which I have prescribed for you].

The next day he went up and expounded [this very prescription] in the study house. She heard about it and choked on a bone (but some say: she converted to Judaism). —YERUSHALMI ABODAH ZARAH 2:2 III

To gain his end, a sage might lie and dissemble.

There were two holy men in Ashqelon, who would eat together, drink together, and study Torah together. One of them died, and he was not properly mourned. But when Bar Maayan, the village tax-collector, died, the whole town took time off to mourn him. The surviving holy man began to weep, saying: Woe, for [the enemies of] Israel will have nothing.

[The deceased holy man] appeared to him in a dream, and said to him: Do not despise the sons of your Lord. This one did one sin, and the other one did one good deed, and it went well for the latter [on earth, so while on earth I was punished for my one sin, he was rewarded for his one good deed].

Now what was the culpable act which the holy man had done? Heaven forfend! He committed no culpable act in his entire life. But one time he [in error] put on the head-phylactery before that of the hand.

Now what was the meritorious deed which Bar Maayan, the village tax-collector, had done? Heaven forfend! He never did a meritorious deed in his life. But once he made a banquet for the councillors of his town, but they did not come. He said: Let the poor come and eat the food, so that it not go to waste.

There are, moreover, those who say that he was traveling along the road with a loaf of bread under his arm, and it fell. A poor man went and picked it up, and the tax-collector said nothing to him so as not to embarrass him.

After a few days the [surviving] holy man saw his fellow [in a dream] walking among gardens, orchards, and fountains of water. He saw Bar Maayan, the village tax-collector, with his tongue hanging out by a river. He wanted to reach the river but could not reach it.

He saw Miriam, the daughter of *'LY BSLYM*, [the translation in this context is uncertain—lexicographer Marcus Mordecai Jastrow defined this as "the leek-like sprouts of onions."] hanging by the nipples of her breasts. Rabbi Yose ben Hanina said: The pin of the gate of Gehenna was fastened to her ear.

[*There follows a conversation between the two holy men, the survivor and the deceased.*]

[The survivor] said to him: Why are things this way? He said to him: Because she fasted and told people about it.

And some say that she fasted one day and had blood drawn on two.

He said to him: And how long will it be this way for her? They [the deceased] said to him: Until Simeon ben Shetah will come, and we shall remove it from her ear and set it in his ear!

He said to him: And what is [Simeon's] crime? They said to him: Because he vowed: If I am made patriarch, I shall kill off all the witches. And, lo, he has been made patriarch, but he has not killed off the witches. Lo, there are eighty witches in a cave of Ashqelon, bringing destruction to the world, so go and tell him.

He said to him: He is a great man, and he will not believe me. He said to him: He is humble, go and he will believe you. Now if he does not believe you, do this as your sign before him: Put your hand in your eye and remove [your eye], and hold it in your hand.

He took out his eye and put it in his hand. They said to put it back, and he put it back beside the other. He went and reported the incident to [Simeon]. He wanted to do the sign for him, but [Simeon] would not allow him to do so. He said to him: I know you are a holy man. Furthermore, I did not say publicly [that I would uproot witchcraft], but I only thought about it [so I know your knowledge comes from Heaven].

Forthwith Simeon ben Shetah arose. Now that day it was raining. Simeon ben Shetah took with him eighty young men and dressed them in eighty clean cloaks. He took with them eighty new pots, with covers. He said to them: When I whistle once, put on your garments. When I whistle a second time, all of you come out at once. When each of you comes out, lift up one of the [witches], and hold her off the ground, because the witchcraft [of those women] does not work if their feet are not touching the ground.

When he went and came to the mouth of the cave, he said: Hello, hello! Open up for me. I am one of yours.

They said to him: How did you come on such a rainy day? He replied: I ran between the raindrops. They said to him: And what did you come here to do? He said to them: To learn and to teach.

When he came in, one of them said something and produced bread. One of them said something and produced cooked food. One of them said something and produced wine. They said to him: And what can you do?

He said to them: I can whistle twice and produce eighty handsome young men, dressed in clean clothes, who will have pleasure with you and give you pleasure too. They said to him: We want them! We want them!

He whistled once, and [the eighty men] put on their clean clothes. He whistled a second time, and they all came out at once. He signaled to them: Each one of you pick a partner and lift her up off the ground.

At that point whatever the witch could do would not work. He said to the one who produced bread: Bring forth bread. But she could produce none. He said: Take her and crucify her.

[He said to the one who produced cooked food:] Bring forth cooked food. But she could not produce, and he said: Take her and crucify her.

[He said to the one who produced wine:] Bring forth wine. But she could not do it, and he said: Take her and crucify her.

And so he did to all of them. This is the background of that which we have learned: **Eighty women did Simeon ben Shetah hang in Ashqelon. They do not judge two capital cases on the same day** Mishnah Sanhedrin 6:6: but the times required it. —YERUSHALMI HAGIGAH 2:2 V

Clearly the status of the victims in some of these stories accounts for the Yerushalmi's treatment of these actions as exemplary which we should regard as disreputable. You may lie to a sorcerer or a witch, for example. Still, since we seek images of humanity for our own day and not for a day long gone alone, we are right to regard the tales at hand as representations of a less-than-noble ideal.

Nor should we take for granted that the storytellers' judgment accords with the opinion of sages in general. The concept, for example, that the end justifies the means did not find universal acceptance. A rabbi who saved many by handing over a few was not praised, and the storyteller made it clear that general opinion opposed such pusillanimous behavior.

It is taught: [As to] a group of men to whom gentiles said: Give us one of your number that we may kill him, and if not, lo, we will kill all of you Tosefta Terumot 7:20—let them kill all of them, but let them not give over to them a single Israelite.

But if they singled one out [by name], such as they singled out Sheba the son of Bichri [2 Samuel 20]—let them give him to them, that they not all be killed.

Said Rabbi Simeon ben Laqish: Now this [latter ruling] applies [only] if the man [already] is subject to execution, as was Sheba the son of Bichri.

But Rabbi Yohanan said: [It applies] even if he is not subject to execution, as was Sheba the son of Bichri.

[An example is given of Simeon ben Laqish's view.] Ulla bar Qushab—the government wanted him [for a sentence of death]. He fled and went to Lod [where he was] near Rabbi Joshua ben Levi. [The agents of the king] came and surrounded the town. They said: If you do not give him to us, we will destroy the town.

Rabbi Joshua ben Levi went to [Ulla] and convinced him [to give himself up]. So [Joshua] turned him over to them.

Now [until then the prophet] Elijah (may his memory be for good!) had been accustomed to reveal himself to [Joshua ben Levi]. [When Elijah came no more, Joshua] fasted several times. [As a result, Elijah] revealed himself to him. [Elijah] said to him: Should I reveal myself to informers, [who deliver Jews into the hands of the government]?

[Joshua] said to him: [I am no traitor.] Did I not [simply] carry out [a rule of] the law? [Elijah] said to him: Is this indeed the law for pious ones?! [Surely not.] —YERUSHALMI TERUMOT 8:10 II [Translated by Alan S. Avery-Peck]

... BUT STILL OF MORTAL NATURE

The sage remained, in heart and soul and in character, at one with the rest of the Israelite sector of humanity. Yet his virtue lay in understanding that fact, recognizing that whatever supernatural gifts he might enjoy came from God. If tales reported that sages could make rain, some of these same stories also stressed that more often than not God responded to the moral condition of the community, not to the special pleading of the sage.

There was a pestilence in Sepphoris, but it did not come into the neighborhood in which Rabbi Hanina was living. And the Sepphoreans said: How is it possible that the Elder lives among you, he and his entire neighborhood, in peace, while the town goes to ruin?

[Hanina] went in and said before them: There was only a single Zimri [Numbers 25] in his generation, but on his account, twenty-four thousand people died. And in our time, how many Zimris are there in our generation? And yet you are raising a clamor!

One time they had to call a fast, but it did not rain. Rabbi Joshua carried out a fast in the South, and it rained. The Sepphoreans said: Rabbi Joshua ben Levi brings down rain for the people in the South, but Rabbi Hanina holds back rain for us in Sepphoris.

They found it necessary to declare a second time of fasting, and sent and summoned Rabbi Joshua ben Levi. [Hanina] said to him: Let my lord go forth with us to fast.

The two of them went out to fast, but it did not rain. [Hanina] went in and preached to them as follows: It was not Rabbi Joshua ben Levi who brought down rain for the people of the South, nor was it Rabbi Hanina who held back rain from the people of Sepphoris. But as to the Southerners, their hearts are open, and when they listen to a teaching of Torah they submit [to accept it], while as to the Sepphoreans, their hearts are hard, and when they hear a teaching of Torah they do not submit [or accept it].

When he went in, he looked up and saw that the [cloudless] air was pure. He said: Is this how it still is? [Is there no change in the weather?]

Forthwith, it rained. He took a vow for himself that he would never do the same thing again. He said: How shall I tell the creditor [God] not to collect what is owing to Him? —YERUSHALMI TAANIT 3:4 I

Accordingly, supernatural intervention followed moral regeneration of the community at large, just as the rabbis were telling all Israel concerning the national yearning for the Messiah. It was a single message, in a number of diverse media. The sage needed the fellowship of the community.

Judah of Husa hid in a cave for three days to inquire into the reason for the rule that the maintenance of the life of this town takes precedence over the maintenance of the life of another town. He came to Rabbi Yose ben Halafta, saying to him: I hid in a cave for three days to inquire into the reason for the rule that the maintenance of the life of this town takes precedence over the maintenance of the life of another town.

He called Rabbi Abba, his son, saying to him: What is the reason for the rule that the maintenance of the life of this town takes precedence over the maintenance of the life of another town?

He recited for him the following verse: These cities had each its pasture lands round about it; so it was with all these cities Joshua 21:42. [That is, each city was supplied with all its needs.]

He said to him: What caused your ignorance? It was that you did not study with your fellow [but all by yourself]. —YERUSHALMI NEDARIM 11:1 IV

Recognizing the higher claim of the community, the sage submitted to the judgment of his peers and accepted deposition, even from the highest office, when publicly rebuked.

A certain student came and asked Rabbi Joshua: What is the law about the evening prayer? He said to him: Optional.

[The student] came and asked Rabban Gamaliel: What is the law about the evening prayer? He said to him: Compulsory.

[The student] said to him: But Rabbi Joshua said: Optional!

[Rabban Gamaliel] said to him: Tomorrow, when I come into the meetinghouse, get up and ask about this law.

The next day that same student got up and asked Rabban Gamaliel: What is the law about the evening prayer? He said to him: Compulsory. He said: But Rabbi Joshua said: Optional.

Rabban Gamaliel said to Rabbi Joshua: Is it you who says: Optional? He said: No.

[Rabban Gamaliel] said to him: Stand on your feet, and let them bear witness against you.

And Rabban Gamaliel sat and expounded, and Rabbi Joshua remained standing, until all the people shouted and said to Rabbi Huspit the *meturgeman:* Dismiss the assembly!

They said to Rabbi Zenun the Hazzan: Say ...

He began to speak. All the people began to get up and say to [Gamaliel]: For upon whom has not come your unceasing evil? Nahum 3:19.

They went and appointed Rabbi Eleazar ben Azariah into the Academy. He was sixteen years old, and all his hair turned gray. Rabbi Aqiba was sitting sorrowfully and saying: Not that he is more learned than I, but he is of more illustrious parentage than I. Happy the man whose fathers have gained him merit! Happy the man who has a peg upon whom to hang!

And what was Rabbi Eleazar ben Azariah's peg? He was the tenth generation in descent from Ezra.

And how many benches were there? Rabbi Jacob ben Sisi said: There were eighty benches there, of students, besides those standing behind the fence. Rabbi Yose ben Rabbi Abun said: There were 300, besides those standing behind the fence. [This is the reference of] what we learn elsewhere: **On the day they seated Rabbi Eleazar ben Azariah in the Academy** Mishnah Zebahim 1:3; Mishnah Yadaim 3:5; 4:2.

We learn elsewhere: **This is a midrash which Rabbi Eleazar ben Azariah expounded before the sages at the Vineyard in Yabneh** Mishnah Ketubot 4:6. But was there a vineyard there? Rather, these are the students who were arranged in rows, as in a vineyard.

Rabban Gamaliel immediately went to the home of each person to appease him. He went to Rabbi Joshua; he found him sitting making needles. He said to him: Are these how you make your living? [Joshua] said: And are you just now trying to find out? Woe to the generation of which you are the steward. Rabban Gamaliel said to him: I submit to you.

And they sent a certain laundry-worker to Rabbi Eleazar ben Azariah. But some say it was Rabbi Aqiba. [The messenger] said to him: The sprinkler, son of a sprinkler, should sprinkle; shall he that is neither a sprinkler nor the son of a sprinkler say to the sprinkler, son of a sprinkler: Your water comes from a cave, and your ashes from roasting?

[Rabbi Eleazar ben Azariah] said to them: Are you satisfied? You and I shall wait at Rabban Gamaliel's door.

Nonetheless, they did not depose [Rabbi Eleazar ben Azariah] from his high dignity, but rather appointed him *Ab Bet Din* [head of the court]. —YERUSHALMI TAANIT 4:1 XIV [Translated by Shamai Kanter in *Rabban Gamaliel II: The Legal Traditions* (Chicago, 1980), pp. 18-19.]

In the end, it took superhuman power for the sage to accept his standing without the reassurance of the community at large.

Said Rabbi Ba: At first each one would appoint his own disciples [to the court]. For example, Rabbi Yohanan ben Zakkai appointed Rabbi Eliezer and Rabbi Joshua; Rabbi Joshua appointed Rabbi Aqiba; and Rabbi Aqiba, Rabbi Meir and Rabbi Simeon.

[Aqiba] said: Let Rabbi Meir take his seat first.

Rabbi Simeon's face turned pale.

Rabbi Aqiba said to him: Let it be enough for you that I and your Creator recognize your powers. —YERUSHALMI SANHEDRIN 1:1 XII

So the sage stands before us, warts and all: like God, like a demon, but mainly, like mortals in all their frailty and need for the tender gift of love, the tribute of another's esteem.

7

Our Sages in Society

SAGES FORMED A SOCIALLY and politically distinct group. True, they also participated in the collective life of Israel. But their group was socially distinguished by the disciplines they alone carried out: in the intellect, the life of Torah-learning in particular; and in the streets, the life of the relationship of master and disciple. What made a man a sage was not mere knowledge, but knowledge acquired through discipleship and expressed in a distinctive pattern of thought and behavior. The sages as a group were politically distinguished by their inner discipline, their adherence to a particular viewpoint and policy for the Jewish nation at large, and their constant search for position in such Jewish government as existed. Sages were too few to be called a social class, but too many to be regarded as isolated and ineffectual, a merely cultural phenomenon. Seen in retrospect, they formed the clerical estate; they compared in their defined traits to the castes into which Israel had divided itself, and in some ways they constituted a political movement. In calling them an estate, I take account of the society they formed within the larger Jewish nation.

The Talmud's critical actor is the rabbi, as authority on earth and as intermediary of supernatural power. If we did not know the time and place from which the Talmud comes, knowledge of those two definitive facts of this document, coupled with familiarity with the world of late antiquity, should have enabled us to guess it. For the rabbi, so particular to Judaism and distinctive to the Talmud, also is typical of his age. He presents a version, in Judaism, of what was wholly commonplace in the world at large. This is how Peter Brown describes matters (*World*, pp. 102-103):

> The idea of the holy man holding the demons at bay and bending the will of God by his prayers came to dominate Late Antique society. In many ways, the idea is as new as the society itself. For it placed a man, a "man of power," in the centre of people's imagination.

This chapter focuses on the rabbi in society, in the society of those closest to him, his colleagues and disciples, then in expanding circles outward, to pious men, to ordinary folk, and, finally, to women.

THE SAGES' ESTATE

Whether we can call the sages a social class depends upon what we mean by a class. Definitions vary greatly, so the matter is scarcely clear. But we can regard the sages as a clearly identifiable social group, because they followed a single program of concerns and policies and, in the main, exercised remarkable discipline among themselves. The means of enforcing this discipline flowed from the character and convictions of the group. Sages stressed the importance of relating to one another—as disciples of a master, as fellow students of the law—therefore the principal sanction lay in exclusion from the company of sages. Since the cause of estrangement derived from the law and debates about it, and since, furthermore, rabbis claimed to exercise supernatural power, we can hardly be surprised at the story of Eliezer's excommunication. It contains the principal tensions and their resolution: tensions among sages about social norms, that is, laws; conflict between nature and supernature in the resolution of the law.

They sought to excommunicate Rabbi Eliezer. They said: Who will go and inform him? Rabbi Aqiba said: I shall go and inform him.

He came to him. He said to him: Rabbi, see, your colleagues are excommunicating you.

[Eliezer] took him and went outside. He said: O carob, carob, if the law accords with their view, uproot yourself. And [the carob tree] did not uproot itself.

[Eliezer said:] If the law is according to my view, uproot yourself. And it uprooted itself.

[He spoke again to the tree, saying:] If the law accords with their view, return [to your place]. And it did not return.

[He said:] If the law accords with my view, return to your place. And it returned.

All such praise and the law is not according to Rabbi Eliezer?

Hanina said: Once [the law] has been given, it has been given only on condition that one follows the majority, even [when the majority is] in error.

And does Rabbi Eliezer not accept the principle that one follows the majority, even in error?

[Eliezer] paid no attention [to the majority] until in his very presence they burned the things he had declared clean. There we have learned: **If he broke it into rings and put sand between the rings—Rabbi Eliezer declares clean. And sages declare unclean. This is the oven of Hakhinai** Mishnah Kelayim 5:10.

Rabbi Jeremiah said: A great tribulation took place on that day. Wherever Rabbi Eliezer's eye looked, [what he gazed upon] was burned, and not only so, but even one grain of wheat—the half [that he looked at] was burned, and [the other] half not burned.

And the columns of the assembly-house were shaking. Rabbi Joshua said to [the columns]: If the associates [the sages] are contending, what business is it of yours? And an echo came forth and said: The law follows my son, Eliezer.

Rabbi Joshua said: **It is not in Heaven** Deuteronomy 30:12.

Rabbi Qerispai, Rabbi Yohanan in the name of Rabbi: If a man should say to me: Thus did Rabbi Eliezer teach . . . I should teach according to his words, but the Tannas confuse matters. [The teachings of Eliezer are not accurately attributed to him.]

One time [Eliezer] was going through the market and he saw one woman cleaning her house, and she threw out [the dirt] and it fell on his head. He said: It would seem that today my colleagues will draw me near, as it is written: From the dung heap He will raise up the poor Psalms 113:7. —YERUSHALMI MOED QATAN 3:1 VI

From the point of view of the sages, of course, their estate took precedence over the conventional castes.

A sage takes precedence over a king; a king takes precedence over a high priest; a high priest takes precedence over a prophet; a prophet takes precedence over a priest anointed for war; a priest anointed for war takes precedence over the head of a priestly watch; the head of a priestly watch takes precedence over the head of a household [of priests]; the head of a household of priests takes precedence over the superintendant of the cashiers; the superintendant of the cashiers takes precedence over the Temple treasurer; the Temple treasurer takes precedence over an ordinary priest; an ordinary priest takes precedence over a Levite; a Levite takes precedence over an Israelite; an Israelite takes precedence over a *mamzer* [illegitimate child]; a *mamzer* takes precedence over a *natin* [slave]; a *natin* takes precedence over a proselyte; a proselyte takes precedence over a freed slave Tosefta Horayyot 2:1.

Under what circumstances? When all of them are equivalent. But if a mamzer **was the disciple of a sage, and a high priest was an ignoramus, the** mamzer **who is the disciple of a sage takes precedence over a high priest who is an ignoramus** Mishnah Horayyot 3:5.

A sage takes precedence over a king. [For if] a sage dies, we have none who is like him. [If] a king dies, any Israelite is suitable to mount the throne Tosefta Horayyot 2:8.

Said Rabbi Yohanan: All those forty days that Moses served on the mountain, he studied the Torah but forgot it. In the end it was given to him as a gift. All this, why? So as to bring the stupid students back to their studies [when they become discouraged].

When Rabbi Simon bar Zebid died, Rabbi Hili went up to take leave of him [with these words]: Surely there is a mine for silver, and a place for gold which they refine. Iron is taken out of the earth, and copper is smelted from the ore. Job 28:1-2. These, if

they are lost, can be replaced. But a disciple of a sage who dies —
who will bring someone to take his place? But where shall wisdom
be found? And where is the place of understanding? Man does
not know the way to it, and it is not found in the land of the living
Job 28:12-13.

Said Rabbi Levi: If the hearts of Joseph's brothers failed them
because they found something, as it is written: At this their hearts
failed them Genesis 42:28, we who have lost Rabbi Simeon bar Zebid,
how much the more so! —YERUSHALMI HORAYYOT 3:5 I

SAGES AND DISCIPLES

*In fact, the Yerushalmi refers not so much to sages as to disciples
of sages, and discipleship defined the social norm. Few reached
the position of acknowledged masters, but many competed to serve
those few and to attain knowledge of the Torah through that service. It involved memorizing sayings repeated as authoritative rules
by the master, and also imitating the deeds of the master. These
deeds, properly framed in words of general import, served as legal
precedents at least as authoritative as memorized sentences
attributed to the authority of earlier masters. Entry into discipleship brought the disciple into a supernatural relationship that
replaced natural ones: the sage replaced the father; the company
of disciples and master, the family. The power of the Torah was such
as to impose upon the disciple the responsibilities, duties, and obligations owing from the son to the father, hence, a transformation
of natural into supernatural relationships. That is why when his
master died, a disciple had to perform the formal rites of mourning owing to a parent.*

Just as they make a tear [in the garment, as a sign of mourn-
ing] for sages, so they make a tear for their disciples. What is the
definition of a disciple of a sage? Hezekiah said: It is any one who
has learned laws and [their basis in the law of Torah] in addition.

Rabbi Yose said to him: That which you have said applies in
the beginning. But as to nowadays, even if one has learned only
laws [that, too, qualifies such a person for the title of disciple of
a sage].

Rabbi Abbahu in the name of Rabbi Yohanan: It is anyone who sets aside his worldly affairs on account of his learning of Mishnah.

It was taught: It is anyone whom they ask a question and who can answer it. Said Rabbi Hoshaia: Take us, for example, for our masters inspect our learning, and we are able to answer them.

Said Rabbi Ba bar Mamel: It is anyone who knows how to explain what he has learned in the Mishnah. But as to us, even our masters do not know how to explain the Mishnah that we have learned.

[In the Tosefta's version:] Who is one's master? [Yerushalmi omits:] It is the one who has taught him wisdom [and not the master who has taught him a trade]. —YERUSHALMI MOED QATAN 3:7 IV

One therefore had to know just who his master was.

Who is one's master? It is the one who has taught him wisdom [and not the master who has taught him a trade]. It is anyone who started him off first—the words of Rabbi Meir. Rabbi Judah says: It is anyone from whom he has gained the greater part of his learning. Rabbi Yose says: It is anyone who has enlightened his eyes in his repetition of traditions Tosefta Horayyot 2:5.

Rabbi Abbahu came [and taught] in the name of Rabbi Yohanan: The law is in accordance with the position of the one who says: It is anyone from whom he has gained the greater part of his learning. (Now why did he not simply interpret the Mishnah-pericope by saying: The law is in accord with Rabbi Judah? [Because there are] repeaters of traditions who will get confused and switch [masters about].)

Rabbi Eliezer would make a tear in mourning on the demise of someone who had simply opened his education at the outset [but was not his principal teacher].

Samuel removed his phylacteries on the news of the demise of one who had enlightened his eyes in his learning of the Mishnah.

And what is the case of one's **enlightening his eyes in his learning of the Mishnah?** It is one who taught merely so brief a passage as the following: **[The two keys]—one goes down into the lock as far as its armpit, and one opens the door forthwith** Mishnah Tamid 3:6. (Now what is the meaning of **One goes down into**

the lock as far as its armpit? That it would go down for a cubit before it would open the door.)

Rabbi Hananiah was walking, leaning on the shoulder of Rabbi Hiyya bar Ba in Sepphoris. He saw all the people running. He asked him: Why do all the people run? [Hiyya] said to him: It is because Rabbi Yohanan is in session and expounding Torah in the schoolhouse of Rabbi Benaiah, and all the people are running to hear what he has to say.

[Hananiah] said to him: Blessed be the All-Merciful, who has shown me the fruits of my labor while I am still alive. For [Hananiah] had laid forth before [Yohanan] all of the Aggadah, except for Proverbs and Ecclesiastes. [Yohanan had been his disciple.] —YERUSHALMI HORAYYOT 3:4 IV

SAGES AND PIOUS FOLK

Beyond the disciples' inner circle was a circle formed by pious folk, whose piety consisted in devoting their money to the support of masters and disciples. They did so because of their devotion to the Torah, of course, but they could thereby hope to gain even this-worldly response.

Rabbi Eliezer, Rabbi Joshua, and Rabbi Aqiba went up to Holat Antokhiya in connection with collecting funds for sages. Now there was a certain man there, by the name of Abba Judah. He would fulfill the commandment [of supporting the sages] in a liberal spirit. One time he lost all his money, and he saw our rabbis and despaired [of helping them]. He went home, and his face was filled with suffering.

His wife said to him: Why is your face filled with suffering? He said to her: Our rabbis are here, and I simply do not know what I can do for them.

His wife, who was even more righteous than he, said to him: You have a single field left. Go and sell half of it and give the proceeds to them.

He went and did just that. He came to our rabbis, and he gave them the proceeds. Our rabbis prayed in his behalf. They said to him: Abba Judah, may the Holy One, blessed be He, make up all the things you lack.

When they went their way, he went down to plough the half-field that remained in his possession. Now while he was plough-ing in the half-field that remained to him, his cow fell and broke a leg. He went down to bring her up, and the Holy One, blessed be He, opened his eyes, and he found a jewel. He said: It was for my own good that my cow broke its leg.

Now when our rabbis returned, they asked about him. They said: How are things with Abba Judah?

People replied: Who can [even] gaze upon the face of Abba Judah—Abba Judah of the oxen! Abba Judah of the camels! Abba Judah of the asses!

So Abba Judah had returned to his former wealth. Now he came to our rabbis and asked after their welfare. They said to him: How is Abba Judah doing?

He said to them: Your prayer in my behalf has yielded fruit and more fruit. They said to him: Even though, to begin with, other people gave more than you did, you were the one whom we wrote down at the top of the register.

They took and seated him with themselves, and they pro-nounced him the following scriptural verse: A man's gift makes room for him and brings him before great men Proverbs 18:16. — YERUSHALMI HORAYYOT 3:4 III

A disciple of means could not suffice merely through his life of learning; he had the further obligation to give over his wealth to support the masters of Torah.

Rabbi Aha in the name of Rabbi Tanhum ben Rabbi Hiyya: If one has learned, taught, kept, and carried out [the Torah], and he has ample means in his possession to strengthen the Torah and he did not do so, lo, such a one still is in the category of those who are cursed. [The meaning of "to strengthen" here is to support the masters of Torah.]

Rabbi Jeremiah in the name of Rabbi Hiyya bar Ba: [If] one did not learn, teach, keep, and carry out [the teachings of the Torah], but did not have ample means to strengthen [the masters of the Torah, but nonetheless he did strengthen them], lo, such a one falls into the category of those who are blessed.

And Rabbi Hannah, Rabbi Jeremiah in the name of Rabbi Hiyya: The Holy One, blessed be He, is going to prepare a protection for those who carry out religious duties [of support for masters of Torah] through the protection afforded to the masters of Torah [themselves].

What is the scriptural basis for that statement? For the protection of wisdom is like the protection of money Ecclesiastes 7:12. And it says: [The Torah] is a tree of life to those who lay hold of it; those who hold it fast are called happy Proverbs 3:18. —YERUSHALMI SOTAH 7:4 IV

Sages, for their part, acknowledge obligations to pious folk. Those who kept the law as the sages taught it had the right to demand sages' support.

There was a case of thirteen brothers, twelve of whom died childless. The surviving levirate widows came and brought their case before Rabbi. Rabbi said to the last brother: Go and enter into levirate marriage with them.

He said to him: I don't have the resources to support them.

They replied: Each one of us will provide maintenance for a month [each year].

He said: And who will provide for the intercalated month [in leap years]?

Said Rabbi: I shall provide for the intercalated month.

He prayed for them, and they went their way. Three years later they came, accompanied by thirty-six children.

They came and told Rabbi: There's a whole town of children down there, who want to greet you.

Rabbi looked out the window and saw them. He said to them: What is your business with me?

They said to him: We want you to provide maintenance for us for the intercalated month.

He provided food for them for the intercalated month. — YERUSHALMI YEBAMOT 4:12 II

SAGES AND
ORDINARY PEOPLE

The sages' judgment of ordinary people — that is, Jews not part of their disciple-master circles and not responsive to their influence — proves complex. They denigrated as worthless any learning not acquired through the discipline of discipleship. As the following example shows, whatever one knew could not be right, and that by definition.

He who finds a neglected corpse, lo, this one must attend to him and bury him where he lies.

Under what circumstances? When he has found him outside of the boundary of a town. But if he found [the corpse] within the boundary of the town, lo, this one brings him to the place of burial and buries him [in the normal cemetery].

Said Rabbi Aqiba: Thus was the beginning of my labor of learning before sages. One time I was walking along the way, and I found a neglected corpse, and I attended to him for about four *mils*, until I brought him to the graveyard, and I buried him there. Now when I came to Rabbi Eliezer and to Rabbi Joshua, I told them what I had done. They said to me: For every step you took, you were credited as if you had shed blood [for taking the neglected corpse away from the spot in which he should have been buried]. Now I said: If when I intended to acquire merit, I suffered blame [for not doing things correctly], when I do not intend to acquire merit, how much the more so [do I suffer blame]. From that time I have not ceased to serve [and study with] sages.

[Aqiba] would say: He who does not serve sages is worthy of death. —YERUSHALMI NAZIR 7:1 XIII

The sages further regarded the piety of outsiders as null, even though they acknowledged the contingent value of that piety. Prayer was obviously approved, but prayer was less important than Torah-study in the cultic-ritual framework of the master-disciple circle. Therefore, spending money on synagogues did not gain the sages' approval. The money should rather go to support disciples and their masters.

Rabbi Hama bar Hanina and Rabbi Hoshaia the Elder were strolling in the synagogues in Lud. Said Rabbi Hama bar Hanina to Rabbi Hoshaia: How much money did my forefathers invest here [in building these synagogues]!

He said to him: How many lives did your forefathers invest here! Were there not people who were laboring in Torah [who needed the money more]?

Rabbi Abun made the gates of the great hall [of study]. Rabbi Mana came to him. [Abun] said to him: See what I have made!

He said to him: For Israel has forgotten his Maker and built palaces! Hosea 8:14. Were there no people laboring in Torah [who needed the money more]? —YERUSHALMI SHEQALIM 5:4 II

Nor should profits made in business interfere with learning.

A certain rabbi would teach Scripture to his brother in Tyre, and when they came and called him to do business, he would say: I am not going to take away from my fixed time to study. If the profit is going to come to me, let it come in due course [after my fixed time for study has ended]. —YERUSHALMI SOTAH 9:13 VI

People who failed to pay the fees of disciples, such as teachers or scribes, for services these disciples rendered, could look forward only to ruin.

Rabbi Simeon ben Yohai taught: If you see towns which have been uprooted from their original location in the Land of Israel, you should know that the inhabitants did not faithfully pay the fee of the scribes and teachers [who worked there].

What is the scriptural basis for that statement? It is written: Why is the land ruined and laid waste like a wilderness, so that no one passes through? And the Lord says: Because they have forsaken My Torah which I set before them Jeremiah 9:11-12. —YERUSHALMI HAGIGAH 1:7 I

In the sages' view expressed through stories they told, ordinary folk responded in kind. They commanded the livelihoods of disciples of sages who went out to teach in the towns, and when the disciple rejected the policy of the townsfolk, he was fired, as in the first selection below. No wonder then that the disciple might be intimidated, as seen in the second selection.

To Rabbi Simeon, teacher of Trachonitis, the townspeople said: Cut short your reading so that our children may learn to read [by following it slowly].

He came and asked Rabbi Hanina [whether to accept this instruction]. [Hanina] said to him: Even if they cut off your head, do not listen to [obey] them.

So he did not listen to them, and they fired him from his job as teacher. After a while he came down here [to Babylonia, where the story was told]. Rabbi Simon ben Yusinah dealt with him. He said to him: What did you do in that town? And he told him the story.

[Simon] said to him: Why did you not listen to them [and do what they wanted]? He said to him: And do they [the sages] do it that way?

[Simon] said to him: And do we not cut a verse in parts in the study-session [so as to translate it bit by bit and learn it that way]?

[Simeon] said to him: But do we not then go back and say the whole thing as one piece?

Said Rabbi Zeira: If that teacher were alive in my time, I should appoint him as a sage. [He was exemplary, for he carried out the law in the proper manner.] —YERUSHALMI MEGILLAH 4:5 III

There [in Babylonia, where they prepare a writ of *halisah*], they state in the writ: She appeared before us and removed his shoe from his right foot and spit before us with spittle which could be seen on the ground, and she stated: So shall it be done to the man who does not build up his brother's house.

Said Rabbi Abbahu: Once the spit has come out of her mouth, even if the wind picked it up and carried it away, the rite is valid.

[Would it be valid] if she spit blood?

Rabbi Ba in the name of Rabbi Judah, Rabbi Zeriqan introduced the statement [in the name of] Rabbi Jeremiah in the name of Abba bar Abba, Rabbi Zeira introduced the matter in the name of Samuel: If there is any remnant of spittle [in the blood], it is valid.

[What of a case involving] a woman without hands — how does she remove the shoe? With her teeth.

The people of Simonia came before Rabbi. They said to him: We want you to give us a man to serve as preacher, judge, leader [of Scripture], teacher [of tradition], and to do all the things we need. He gave them Levi bar Sisi.

They set up a great stage and seated him on it. They came and asked him: A woman without arms—with what does she remove the shoe? And he did not answer.

They said: Perhaps he is not a master of the law. Let us ask him something about lore.

They came and asked him: What is the meaning of the following verse, as it is written: But I will tell you what is inscribed in the book, in truth Daniel 10:21? If it is truth, why is it described as inscribed? And if it is inscribed, why is it described as truth? He did not answer them.

They came back to Rabbi and said to him: Is this a mason of your mason's guild [a pupil of your school]?

He said to them: By your lives! I gave you someone who is as good as I am.

[Rabbi] sent and summoned [Levi] and asked him. He said to [Levi]: If the woman spit blood, what is the law? He answered him: If there is a drop of spittle in it, it is valid.

[He asked further:] A woman without arms—how does she remove the shoe? He said to him: She removes the shoe with her teeth.

[Rabbi] said to him: What is the meaning of the following verse, as it is written: But I will tell you what is inscribed in the book, in truth? If it is truth, why is it desribed as inscribed, and if it is inscribed, why is it described as truth? [Levi] said to him: Before a decree is sealed, it is described as inscribed. Once it is sealed, it is described as truth.

[Rabbi] said to him: And why did you not answer the people when they asked you these same questions?

[Levi] said to him: They made a great stage and seated me on it, and my spirit became exalted.

[Rabbi] recited concerning [Levi] the following verse of Scripture: If you have been foolish, exalting yourself, or if you have been devising evil, put your hand on your mouth Proverbs 30:32. What caused you to make a fool of yourself in regard to teachings of Torah? It was because you exalted yourself through them.

—YERUSHALMI YEBAMOT 12:6 III-IV

THE SAGES AND WOMEN

Women proved an anomaly. By the time attested in the Yerushalmi, the third and fourth centuries, women were totally excluded from the processes of Torah-study through discipleship. There is not a single instance in the Yerushalmi in which a story is told about a woman who served as a disciple to a master. By the same token, women not only formed half of the Jewish nation but they also formed half of the sages' estate: their wives and daughters. So they cannot fall wholly into the range of complete outsiders, but they also cannot come within the magic circle of the disciples themselves. That constitutes the anomalous character imposed by gender on one-half of all Israel. How did the system to which the Yerushalmi testifies sort out the complex relationships with women, near and far? On the one side, it was clear that women did not fit very well in the caste-world. That is why they moved from caste to caste, as the biblical rules governing priests' wives and daughters show. But, on the other side, the all-male society of masters and disciples had to take into account in some way not only the need for women but also their love, as mothers, wives, and daughters and daughters-in-law, a love that, after all, was reciprocated.

The rules replicate a set of opposites generated by a complex ideology. In the first two examples below, man takes precedence. In the next two, for good and substantial reasons, women enjoy admiration, gratitude, respect, and love. The fifth selection makes it clear that some sages were nothing more than misogynists.

A man takes precedence over a woman. Now that is the rule if **one had this one to save and that one to save, this one to clothe and that one to clothe** Mishnah Horayyot 3:4. [That is, when all things are equal, the man takes precedence in the one instance, the woman in the other.]

Lo, if one had this one to restore to life and that one to clothe [what is the rule]? Let us infer the rule from that which Rabbi Joshua ben Levi said in the name of Rabbi Antigonos: [If there is a choice of] providing a garment for the wife of an associate, and saving the life of an ordinary person, the garment for the wife of the associate takes precedence over saving the life of the ordinary person, on account of the honor owing to the associate.

Now the rule has been stated only with regard to providing a garment for the wife of an associate in the lifetime of the associate. But if it was a case of saving this one and clothing that one, saving the life takes precedence.

[If one has the choice of retrieving] that which he has lost and that which his father has lost, his own takes precedence. [If he has a choice of retrieving] that which he has lost and that which his master has lost, his own takes precedence. [If he has a choice of retrieving] that which his father has lost and that which his master has lost, that of his master takes precedence [over that of his father]. For his father has brought him into this world, but his master, who taught him wisdom, has brought him into the life of the world to come
Mishnah Baba Mesia 2:11.

[Under discussion is] his master who taught him the Mishnah, not his master who taught him the Scripture.

Now if his father was the equal of his master, his father takes precedence. What is the difference favoring [the father]?

Said Rabbi Yose ben Rabbi Bun: It is a case in which half of his learning came from this one, and half of his learning came from that one [, so the father's having brought him into the world gains precedence for the father].

[If it is a choice of retrieving] that which his father, from whom he had acquired half of his learning, has lost, and that which his mother, whom his father has divorced, has lost, who takes precedence? Is it the father who takes precedence? Or [does the father take precedence] only when the whole of the man's learning has derived from the father?

Is it his master who takes precedence, or [is this the case] only when all of his learning has come from the master?

[If it is a choice of retrieving] that which he has lost, that which his mother has lost, that which his father has lost, and that which his master has lost, that which he has lost takes precedence over that which his father has lost, that which his father has lost takes precedence over that which his mother has lost, and that which his mother has lost takes precedence over that which his master has lost.

Now is this teaching not made explicit in the Mishnah: **A man takes precedence over the woman in the matter of the saving of life and in the matter of returning lost property**? Mishnah Baba Mesia 2:11.

They had in mind to rule that this is the case when his master is not present at all. So this teaching comes to tell you that the rule applies even when his master is present.

[What is the case if] he, his mother, his master, his father are standing in captivity [and awaiting ransom]? He takes precedence over his mother, and his mother over his master, and his master takes precedence over his father. [So ransoming] his mother takes precedence over all other people Tosefta Horayyot 2:5.

Now does not the Mishnah say this explicitly: **A woman takes precedence over a man in the matter of providing clothing and redemption from captivity**? Mishnah Horayyot 3:4. One might consider ruling that the Mishnah speaks of a case in which his master is not present. So the Mishnah comes to tell you that this is the rule even if his master is present. —YERUSHALMI HORAYYOT 3:4 IV

When both of them are standing in danger of [sexual] defilement, the man takes precedence over the woman Mishnah Horayyot 3:4. Why is this the rule? Because the woman is accustomed to such treatment, but the man is not accustomed to such treatment. —YERUSHALMI HORAYYOT 3:5 V

The tale is told that Rabbi Aqiba made for his wife a golden tiara, and the wife of Rabban Gamaliel was jealous of her. And [Gamaliel] said to her: If you had done what she did, I would have been glad to make one for you. [Aqiba's wife] sold her braids of hair and gave him the proceeds, so that he might labor in the Torah. —YERUSHALMI SHABBAT 6:1 X

Rabbi Yose ben Saul told the story of the following case: There was an incident involving a certain woman, who loved to perform the religious commandments [such as feeding the hungry], while her husband hated to perform them. Now a poor man came along, so she gave him food and he ate. When she sensed that her husband was coming back, she took the poor man away and hid him in the attic. She set food before her husband, and he ate and then fell asleep. A snake came along and supped from the same dish. When her husband woke up from his sleep, he wanted to eat. The man in the attic began to chatter [so warning the husband not to eat the food].

Now does the law not state: If someone was sleeping [in the same room as the food, the food] is permitted? [So why should the man have refrained from eating the food anyhow?]

[The serpent] was wrapped around [the bowl, so there was every reason to believe that the serpent had eaten some of the food].

And is not [the wife] prohibited [to the husband] by reason of having been alone [with the poor man]? Because they are adultresses, and blood is upon their hands Ezekiel 23:45 [meaning, if she is guilty of the one misdeed, she will be guilty of the other]. Because [the poor man] was not suspect in regard to shedding blood [as he would have been had he permitted the husband to eat the poisoned food], so he was not suspect in regard to fornication.
—YERUSHALMI ABODAH ZARAH 2:3 I

A Roman matron asked Rabbi Eliezer: How is it that, though only one sin was committed in connection with the golden calf, those who died were killed by three kinds of execution?

He said to her: Woman has no wisdom except at the distaff, for it is written: And all the women that were wise-hearted did spin with their hands Exodus 35:25.

Hyrcanus, his son, said to him: So as not to answer her with a single teaching from the Torah, you have lost out on three hundred *kors* of tithe per year!

He said to him: Let the teachings of the Torah be burned, but let them not be handed over to women.

When she went out, his disciples said to him: Rabbi, this one you have pushed away. To us, what will you say?

Rabbi Berekhiah, Rabbi Abba bar Kahana in the name of Rabbi Eliezer [said]: Whoever was subject to the testimony of witnesses, and who had been properly admonished, died by a court sentence. Whoever was subject to the testimony of witnesses, but was not given an admonition, was subjected to the ordeal of water that brings the curse, like the unfaithful wife. Whoever had neither witnesses nor an admonition died in the subsequent plague.

Both Rab and Levi bar Sisi say: If a person slaughtered an animal to the golden calf, offered up incense, and poured out a drink offering, he died by a regular court sentence. If he clapped his hands, danced, or played before the calf, he was subjected to the ordeal of the water that brings a curse, like the accused wife. If he merely rejoiced in his heart [at the making of the golden calf], he died in a plague. —YERUSHALMI SOTAH 3:4 VII

Women could master Torah traditions; but these were subordinated women, whose intelligence one did not need to acknowledge.

As to the words in Hebrew for "piecemeal" [*serugim*] and for "purslane" [*halaglagot*], the rabbis were in doubt as to their meaning. Said Rabbi Haggai: The associates were wondering about the meaning of the cited words, and also about whether one who is greater in wisdom or one who is greater in years should take precedence.

They said: Let us go and ask the house of Rabbi. They went up to ask. A servant girl of Rabbi's household came out, and she said to them: Go in in order of years.

They said: Let so-and-so go in first, let so-and-so go in first. They began to go in piecemeal [one by one]. She said to them: Why are you going in *serugim* [piecemeal]?

One of the rabbis was carrying portulaca. They fell from him. She said to him: Rabbi, your *halaglagot* [portulaca] have fallen.

She said to her co-worker: Bring a broom. And she brought a bundle of shoots. [This served to explain the language of Isaiah 14:23 – Rabbi's servant knew the language, having learned it in Rabbi's house, though the sages had not.] —YERUSHALMI MEGILLAH 2:2 I

And, in the end, the actuality of a human relationship could break through the iron casing of ritualized relationships.

Rabbi Jacob ben Aha in the name of Rabbi Yohanan, Rabbi Hela in the name of Rabbi Eleazar [said]: Just as a man is concerned for the honor owing to his widow, so he is concerned for the honor owing to the woman he has divorced.

For Rabbi Jacob ben Aha in the name of Rabbi Eleazar: ... and not to hide yourself from your own flesh ... Isaiah 58:7 — this refers to the woman one has divorced.

The wife of Rabbi Yose the Galilean gave him much grief. Rabbi Eleazar ben Azariah went up to see him. He said to him: Rabbi, divorce her, for she does not respect you. He said to him: Her marriage-settlement is too much for me to pay.

[Eleazar] said to him: I'll give you what you need to pay off her marriage-settlement, so you can divorce her.

He gave him what he needed to settle the marriage-contract, and [Yose] divorced her.

She went and married the town bailiff. He lost all his money and went blind. She would accompany him all over town and lead him [when he went out to beg]. Once the couple made the rounds of the entire town and did not get a thing. He said to her: Isn't there another neighborhood?

She said to him: There is another neighborhood. But my former husband lives there, and I don't have the strength to go there.

He began to beat her. At that moment Rabbi Yose the Galilean happened to come by and heard the disgraceful racket they were making in the marketplace. He took the couple and gave them a place in which to live in one of the houses he owned, and provided food for them all the days of their lives. This was in fulfillment of the verse: And not to hide yourself from your own flesh Isaiah 58:7 — this refers to the woman he has divorced.

Even so, her voice was heard by night, and people heard her saying: Is not the pain I suffered outside my body [in having to collect alms] better than the pain I suffer inside my body [in having to live off the alms of my ex-husband]? —YERUSHALMI KETUBOT 11:3 II

"TORAH" AS
A WAY OF LIFE

The social ideal of the sages centered upon ritual learning, that is, study of Torah not for cognitive purposes alone but as a symbolic action expressive of a mythic conviction. How sages compared their way of life with that of other Jews emerges here in passages given in the Mishnah, the Tosefta, and the Talmud, as indicated, in the version of the Yerushalmi.

[The Mishnah:] **Rabbi Nehorai says: I should lay aside every trade in the world and teach my son only Torah. For a man eats its fruits in this world, and the principal remains for the world to come. But other trades are not that way. When a man gets sick or old or has pains and cannot do his job, lo, he dies of starvation. But with Torah it is not that way. But it keeps him from all evil when he is young, and it gives him a future and a hope when he is old. Concerning his youth, what does it say?** They who wait upon the Lord shall renew their strength Isaiah 40:31. **And concerning his old age, what does it say?** They shall still bring forth fruit in old age Psalms 92:15. **And so it says with regard to the patriarch Abraham, may he rest in peace:** And Abraham was old and well along in years, and the Lord blessed Abraham in all things Genesis 24:1. **We find that the patriarch Abraham kept the entire Torah even before it was revealed, since it says:** Since Abraham obeyed My voice and kept My charge, My commandments, My statutes, and My laws Genesis 26:5.

Rabbi Nehorai says: I should lay aside every trade in the world and teach my son only Torah. For they eat the fruit of labor in Torah in this world, but the principal remains for the world to come. For every sort of trade which there is in the world serves a man only when he is young, when he yet has his strength. **But when he falls ill or grows old or has pains, and does not work any more, in the end does he die of starvation. But Torah** is not so. But it honors him and **keeps a man from all evil when he is young and gives him a future and a hope when he is old. When he is young, what does it say?** They who wait upon the Lord shall renew their strength. **And concerning his old age, what does it say?** They shall bring forth fruit in old age Mishnah Qiddushin 4:14, Tosefta Qiddushin 5:16.

And so you find with regard to Abraham, our father, that he kept the Torah even before it had come into the world, as it is said: ... because Abraham obeyed My voice and kept My charge, My commandments, My statutes, and My Torahs Genesis 26:5. So also [the Torah] made him great and blessed him when he was young, and gave him a future and a hope when he was old.

When he was young, what does it say? Now Abraham was very rich in cattle, in silver, and in gold Genesis 13:2.

And when he was old, what does it say? Now Abraham was old, well along in years, and the Lord had blessed Abraham in all things Genesis 24:1.

Rabbi Hezekiah, Rabbi Kohen in the name of Rab: It is forbidden to live in a city in which there are no physician, no bath, and no court to administer floggings and imprison people.

Said Rabbi Yose ben Rabbi Bun: Also it is forbidden to live in a town in which there is no vegetable garden.

Rabbi Hezekiah, Rabbi Kohen in the name of Rab: In the future a man is going to have to give an account of himself for everything which his eye saw and which he did not eat.

Rabbi Eleazar took account of this teaching and set aside funds to purchase every species at least once a year. —YERUSHALMI QIDDUSHIN 4:12 I

8
Our Sages and Israel

THE TALMUD OF THE LAND OF ISRAEL portrays the rabbi as an effective governing authority over Israel. Yet details of the political portrait time and again contradict its main lines. The rabbi was part of the administration of the patriarch, a man who stood at the margins of the rabbinical estate, one foot in, the other out. The power of the sage was further limited by popular will and consensus, by established custom, and by other sorts of Jewish authorities. Furthermore, the rabbi as clerk and bureaucrat dealt with matters of surpassing triviality, a fair portion of them of no probable interest to anyone but a rabbi. He might decide which dog a flea might bite. But would the fleas listen to him? Accordingly, the Yerushalmi, with its voluminous evidence of the rabbis' quest for authority over the Jewish nation, in actuality presents ambiguities about inconsequential concerns. On the one side, the rabbi could make some practical decisions. On the other, he competed for authority over Israel with the patriarch and with local village heads. In the broadest sense, no single Jew decided much.

From the viewpoint of the Roman Empire, moreover, the rabbi was apt to have been one among many sorts of invisible men, self-important nonentities, treating as consequential things that concerned no one but themselves, doing little, changing nothing. After all, in the period in which the tales before us were coming to closure and beginning to constitute the Yerushalmi as we know it, the power of the Jewish nation to govern itself grew ever less. Even the authority of the patriarch ended within this period, leaving only the rabbis and their Talmud, legal theory in abundance but legal standing slight indeed. So we discern a certain disproportion between the insistence of the Yerushalmi that rabbis really decided things and established important precedents, and the Yerushalmi's context—both the actual condition of Israel, whom rabbis ruled, and the waning authority of the government of Israel, by whom rabbis were employed.

Once more, one of the Yerushalmi's principal points of emphasis is revealed, on closer inspection, to address head-on, but in a perverse way, the reality of Israel within the now-Christian Roman Empire. The Yerushalmi displays a puzzling indifference to the stunning, world-historical events of its age. Yet silence may also be a response. It is not possible to suppose that the Yerushalmi's framers—by the end of the fourth century, in the aftermath of nearly a century of Christian rule and pagan disaster, of Jewish messianic fervor followed by a heart-breaking debacle—did not recognize that things had changed for the worse. Nor can we maintain for one moment the outlandish possibility that the rabbis had nothing to say about the events of the day, merely pretending nothing was new. They knew. They cared. They judged. But if so, then we can suppose only one of two alternatives. Either the rabbis of the Yerushalmi framed their document in total disregard of the issues of the day or they composed their principal literary monument in complete encounter with those issues and serene certainty of their mastery. By harping on how *they* decided things, by inserting into the processes of legal theory precedents established in their courts, and by representing the life of Israel in such a way that the government of the nation was shown to be entirely within the hands of the nation's learned, legitimate authorities, the Yerushalmi's sages stated quite clearly what they thought was happening. Israel remained Israel, wholly subject to its own law, entirely in control of its own destiny, fully possessed of its own land. Testimony to and vindication of the eternity of Israel lay in the continuing authority of Israel's sages, fully in control of God's law for Israel.

THE SAGES' GOVERNMENT OF ISRAEL

The sages of the Yerushalmi inherited along with the Mishnah the Mishnah's fantastic theory of the government of Israel. That theory posited an orderly series of steps from village to Temple, projecting an appellate procedure upward, and anticipating a reliable arrangement from top to bottom. This is clear in the first selection.

But when the Yerushalmi tells stories about how things actually were, as against how some intellectuals theorized things ought to be, the mass of contradictions referred to above, becomes apparent. In the second selection, the rabbis are discovered complaining that their bribery of Roman officials or Jewish criminals to accept the authority of Jewish courts produces no result, so that they are unable to control the actions of Jews.

It was taught: Said Rabban Simeon ben Gamaliel: At first only priests, Levites, or Israelites suitable for marriage into the priesthood would sign as witnesses on the marriage contracts of women.

Said Rabbi Yose: At first there were dissensions in Israel only in the court of seventy in the hewn-stone chamber [of the Temple in Jerusalem]. And there were other courts of twenty-three in the various towns of the Land of Israel, and there were other courts of three judges each in Jerusalem — one on the Temple mount, and one on the rampart. [If] someone needed to know what the law was, he would go to the court in his town. ([If] there was no court in his town, he would go to the court in the town nearest his.) If they had heard the law, they told him. If not, he and the most distinguished member of that court would come on to the court which was nearest to his town. If they had heard the law, they told him. And if not, they and the most distinguished member of that group would come to the court which was on the Temple mount. If they had heard, they told them, and if not, these and those would go to the high court which was on the rampart. If they had heard, they told them, and if not, these and those would go to the high court which was in the hewn-stone chamber. For from there Torah spreads forth over all Israel, as it is said: Then you shall do according to what they declare to you from that place which the Lord will choose Deuteronomy 17:10.

The court which was in the hewn-stone chamber, even though it consisted of seventy-one members, might not fall below twenty-three. [If] one of them had to go out, he looked around to see whether there would be twenty-three left [after he departed]. If there would be twenty-three left he went out, and if not, he did not go out—unless there would be twenty-three left. And there they remained in session from the time of the daily whole offering of the morning until the time of the daily whole offering at twilight. On Sabbaths and on festivals they came only to the study house which was on the Temple mount. [If] a question was brought before them, if they had heard the answer, they told them. If not, they stood up for a vote. [If] those who acquitted turned out to form the majority, they declared the man innocent. [If] those who convicted formed the majority, they declared the man guilty. [If] those who declared unclean turned out to form the majority, they declared the matter unclean. [If] those who declared the matter clean formed the majority, they declared the matter clean. From there did the law go forth and circulate in Israel.

From the time that the disciples of Shammai and Hillel who had not served their masters so much as was necessary became numerous, dissensions became many in Israel. And from there they sent for and examined everyone who was wise, prudent, fearful of sin, and of good repute, in whom people found pleasure. (They made [anyone who excelled] a judge in his town.) Once he had been made a judge in his town, they promoted him and seated him on the ramparts court, and from there they promoted him and seated him in the court of the hewn-stone chamber. —YERUSHALMI SANHEDRIN 1:4 II

Rabbi Hiyya, Rabbi Yose, [and] Rabbi Immi were engaged in judging [the case of a woman named] Tamar. She went and complained against them to Antiputa, [governor] of Caesarea. The [rabbis] sent and wrote [about it] to Rabbi Abbahu [who lived in Caesarea].

Rabbi Abbahu sent and wrote to them: We have already won over three advocates, Tob Yeled ["Goodchild"], Tob Lamed ["Well-Learned"], and Tarsus [known by their Greek equivalents as] Ebdocus, Eumusus, and Talassios. But Tamar ["bitter"] is bitterness. She abides in her bitterness, and we tried to sweeten her [by a bribe] but in vain has the smelter smelted Jeremiah 6:29 [for gold could not buy her]. —YERUSHALMI MEGILLAH 3:2 III

THE SAGES' SPECIAL STANDING

The sages claimed special standing in the Jewish community, and that allegation, garbed in myth and magic, carried definite rights. In theory, rabbis — masters and disciples — owned synagogues.

Rabbi Joshua ben Levi said: Synagogues and schoolhouses belong to the sages and their disciples.

Rabbi Hiyya bar Yose received [guests] in the synagogue [and lodged them there, using it as private property].

Rabbi Immi instructed the scribes: If someone comes to you with some slight contact with Torah-learning, receive him, his asses, and his belongings. [Allow him to use the synagogue as his hostel for the night.]

Rabbi Berekhiah went to the synagogue in Beisan. He saw someone rinsing his hands and his feet in a fountain [in the courtyard of the synagogue]. He said to him: It is forbidden to you [to do this. It is not public property!]

The next day the man saw [Berekhiah] washing his hands and feet in the fountain [treating the synagogue as if it were his own property]. He said to him: Rabbi, it is permitted to you, and forbidden to me? He said to him: Yes.

He said to [Berekhiah]: Why? He said to him: Because this is what Rabbi Joshua ben Levi said: Synagogues and schoolhouses belong to sages and their disciples. [They are the domain of the sages.]

As to a vestibule [built at the entrance of the synagogue], what is the law about walking through it? Rabbi Abbahu went through the vestibule. Does this indicate that it is permitted?

Said Rabbi Zechariah, son-in-law of Rabbi Levi: There was a teacher sitting with [children], and if Rabbi Abbahu did not go through, he would not let the children go out, [so it was] because of [the needs of] the children. —YERUSHALMI MEGILLAH 3:3 V

Just as rabbis' slaves and servants absorbed Torah-learning and could explain to experts the meaning of obscure words, so these same hangers-on could execute the penalties that rabbis could use, imposing ostracism ("excommunication") as they willed. But so too could thieves.

A serving woman who worked for Bar Pata was passing by a synagogue, and she saw the teacher hit a child more than was necessary. She said to him: That man [referring to him] should be in excommunication.

He came and asked Rabbi Aha [how to deal with what she had said]. [Aha] said to him: You must take account of yourself [in the light of what she said].

That is to say: He who does something which is improper is to be excommunicated.

Rabbi Simeon ben Laqish was guarding figs in a garden. Thieves came and stole them by night. In the end he found out who they were. He said to them: Let them [you] be excommunicated. They said to him: Let that man [you] be subject to a decree of excommunication.

He paid attention to what they had said. He said: They owe me money, but did they owe me their life [that I put them into excommunication]? [Surely not. What I did was wrong.]

He went and ran after them. He said to them: Release me [from the decree of excommunication]. They said to him: Release us, and we shall release you.

That is to say: He who excommunicates him who should not be subjected to excommunication—his act of excommunication still is valid. —YERUSHALMI MOED QATAN 3:1 X

Rabbis might indulge themselves in ways in which others would not, claiming that the press of public business justified the indulgence.

Rabbi Abbahu went down to bathe in the spring of Tiberias, and he would lean on two Goths as his guards. When they started to fall, he helped them up, and that happened twice. They said to him: What's going on? [Why do you have to lean on us at all?] He said to them: [By leaning on you now] I am saving my strength for my old age.

Rabbi Huna did not go down to the meetinghouse [on the festival day, wanting to save his strength, since he did not wish to walk]. Rabbi Qatina asked: And has it not been taught: They may carry infirm folk?

Rabbi Huna instructed the exilarch to go out in a palanquin [on a festival, if he found the walking tiresome]. Rabbi Hisda asked: And has it not been taught: **They do not go out [on the festival day] in a palanquin—all the same are men and women**? Tosefta Yom Tob 3:17. And can a disciple of a sage err in this matter [by assuming that it is permitted when in fact it is forbidden]? And did Rabbi Huna make an error in this matter?

Rabbi Jeremiah instructed Bar Geranti: A physician may be carried in a litter to go to visit the sick on the Sabbath.

Miasha, son of the son of Rabbi Joshua ben Levi, was carried in a litter to go up to give a talk in public on the Sabbath. Said Rabbi Zeriqan to Rabbi Zeira: When you go to the South, ask [whether this matter is permitted].

The question was presented to Rabbi Simon. Rabbi Simon said to them in the name of Rabbi Joshua ben Levi: It is not the end of the matter that it must be a matter of public need [that will permit someone to make use of a litter on the Sabbath, as in the cases just now listed]. But even if there is the possibility that the public will have need [of a person], it is permitted [to make use of a litter]. — YERUSHALMI BESAH 1:7 I

THE SAGES AND THE COMPETITION

The petty privileges surveyed previously mattered little. In things that counted, the rabbis found themselves in competition with a far stronger Jewish government than theirs. It was the government of the patriarch of the Land of Israel (with its counterpart in

Babylonia under the exilarch). The patriarch enjoyed the recognition of Rome and ruled by right and force, not merely persuasion and moral coercion. He did not have to appeal to the people's fear of supernatural or magical retribution, since he could call on his Roman troops to enforce his will and his policy. And sages, for their part, enjoyed authority and official status as rulers only by virtue of their positions in his administration.

But to call the patriarch the sages' political competition is to state matters awry. In fact, from a worldly perspective, sages were petty clerks, employees of the ethnarch of their ethnic group. The ethnarch may have treated sages with respect and accorded them the little dignity they demanded. But when challenged, he was not to be intimidated and readily called up his troops to deal with uppity rabbis.

Rabbi Simeon ben Laqish said: A ruler who has sinned— they administer lashes to him by the decision of a court of three judges.

What is the law as to restoring him to office? Said Rabbi Haggai: By Moses! If we put him back in office, he will kill us!

Rabbi Judah the Patriarch heard of this ruling [of Rabbi Simeon ben Laqish] and was outraged. He sent a troop of Goths to arrest Rabbi Simeon ben Laqish. [Simeon] fled to the Tower. And some say: It was to Kefar Hittayya.

The next day Rabbi Yohanan went up to the meetinghouse, and Rabbi Judah the Patriarch went up to the meetinghouse. [Judah the Patriarch] said to him: Why does my master not state a teaching of Torah?

[Yohanan] began to clap with one hand [only]. [Judah the Patriarch] said to him: Now do people clap with only one hand? [Yohanan] said to him: No, nor is Ben Laqish here [and just as one cannot clap with one hand only, so I cannot teach Torah if my colleague, Simeon ben Laqish, is absent].

[Judah] said to him: Then where is he hidden? He said to him: In the Tower. He said to him: You and I shall go out to greet him. Rabbi Yohanan sent word to Rabbi Simeon ben Laqish: Get a teaching of Torah ready, because the patriarch is coming over to see you.

[Simeon ben Laqish] came forth to receive them and said: The example that you [Judah] set is to be compared to the paradigm of your Creator. For when the All-Merciful came forth to redeem Israel from Egypt, He did not send a messenger of an angel, but the Holy One, blessed be He, Himself came forth, as it is said: For I will pass through the land of Egypt that night Exodus 12:12 — and not only so, but He and His entire retinue. [What other people on earth is like Your people Israel, whom God went to redeem to be His people 2 Samuel 7:23.] Whom the divinity went [in the singular form] is not written here, but whom God went [in the plural, meaning God and all His retinue].

[Judah the Patriarch] said to him: Now why in the world did you see fit to teach this particular statement [that a ruler who has sinned is subject to lashes]?

[Simeon ben Laqish] said to him: Now did you really think that because I was afraid of you, I would hold back the teaching of the All-Merciful: [And lo,] Rabbi Samuel ben Rabbi Isaac said: [Why do you do such things? For I hear of your evil dealings from all the people.] No, my sons, it is no good report that I hear the people of the Lord spreading abroad. [If a man sins against a man, God will mediate for him; but if a man sins against the Lord, who can intercede for him? But they would not listen to the voice of their father, for it was the will of the Lord to slay them] 1 Samuel 2:23-51. [When] the people of the Lord spread about [an evil report about a man], they remove him [even though he is the patriarch].
—YERUSHALMI HORAYYOT 3:1 II

Yose Meoni interpreted the following verse in the synagogue in Tiberias: Hear this, O priests! Hosea 5:1: Why do you not labor in the Torah? Have not the twenty-four priestly gifts [various tithes and offerings the people are obliged to give to priests] been given to you? [So you need not work and can study.] They said to him: Nothing at all has been given to us.

[Yose Meoni said:] And give heed, O House of Israel! Hosea 5:1: Why do you not give the priests the twenty-four gifts concerning which you have been commanded at Sinai? They said to him: The king [meaning the patriarch] takes them all.

[Yose Meoni said:] Hearken, O house of the king! For the judgment pertains to you Hosea 5:1: To you have I said: And this shall be the priests' due from the people, from those offering a sacrifice [whether it be ox or sheep, that] they shall give to the priest the shoulder, the two cheeks, and the stomach Deuteronomy 18:3. I am going to take my seat with them in court and to make a decision concerning them and blot [the kings] out of the world.

Rabbi Yudan the Patriarch heard [about this attack on the rulers] and was very angry. [Yose] feared and fled. Rabbi Yohanan and Rabbi Simeon ben Laqish went up to make peace with [the patriarch].

They said to him: Rabbi, he is a great man. He said to them: Is it possible that everything which I ask of him, he will give to me? They said to him: Yes. [So Yose was called back.]

[Rabbi Yudan the Patriarch] said to [Yose]: What is the meaning of that which is written: For their mother has played the harlot Hosea 2:5. Is it possible that our matriarch, Sarah, was a whore?

[Yose] said to him: As is the daughter, so is her mother. As is the mother, so is the daughter. As is the generation, so is the patriarch. As is the patriarch, so is the generation. As is the altar, so are its priests....

[Rabbi Yudan the Patriarch] said to them: Is it not enough for him that he dishonors me one time not in my presence, but also in my presence he does so these three times! [The three times referred to are the three comparisons above: As is the generation ..., As is the patriarch ..., and As is the altar....]

[Rabbi Yudan the Patriarch] said to [Yose]: What is the meaning of that which is written: Behold, every one who uses proverbs will use this proverb about you: Like mother, like daughter Ezekiel 16:44. Now was our matriarch, Leah, a whore? As it is written: And Dinah went out Genesis 34:1 [like a whore, thus reflecting on her mother].

[Yose] said to him: It is in accord with that which is written: And Leah went out to meet him Genesis 30:16. They compared one going out to the other [and Leah went out to meet her husband, and Dinah learned from this that it was all right to go out, so she went out to meet the daughters of the land; but she was raped]. [This reply was acceptable. The patriarch was appeased.] —YERUSHALMI SANHEDRIN 2:6 V

The rabbis, for their part, could only resort to their ultimate defense: withdrawal, the self-delusion that, in the end, the patriarch did not really matter much.

Rabbi wanted to release the prohibitions of the Sabbatical Year. Rabbi Phineas ben Yair came to him. He said to him: What sort of crop is coming up this year? [Rabbi] said to him: Endives of good quality.

[Again:] What sort of crop is coming up this year? Endives of good quality.

Thereupon Rabbi realized that [Phineas] did not concur with his view. [Rabbi] said to him: Would the Rabbi [Phineas] not care to eat a bite with us today? He said to him: Yes.

When he went down [to eat], he saw the vast herd of mules belonging to Rabbi standing around, [even though it is forbidden to keep herds of small beasts in the Land]. [Phineas] said: Do Jews feed all of these? It is not possible that [Rabbi] will ever see my face again.

[He went home. Members of the household of Rabbi] heard the report [of what Phineas had said]. They went and told Rabbi. He sent [a messenger] to appease Rabbi Phineas. [The messengers] came to the town [of Phineas]. [Phineas] said: The townspeople of my town will stand up for me.

The townspeople went out and encircled [Phineas, so that he would not be seen by the messengers of Rabbi]. The messengers said to them: Rabbi wants to appease him. So they allowed them to pass, and [the townfolk] went their way.

[Phineas] said: My sons will stand up for me.

A fire descended from Heaven and encircled [Phineas]. [The messengers] went back and informed Rabbi.

[Rabbi] said: Since we did not have the merit of seeing him [again] in this world, we shall have the merit of hearing from him in the world to come. —YERUSHALMI TAANIT 3:1

SAGES AND APOSTATES

If the sages could pretend that the powerful patriarch did not really exist or matter, it was because the weapon they did control – namely, the Torah – could overcome his pagan troops. Appealing to a common source of truth, the sages could manipulate or even intimidate this lesser figure, assumed not to know that truth, not to have the access they did to that supernatural power.

But how could the sages cope with apostates from their own group? Such figures could be assumed to know the Torah as well as they did. So the heretic from the sages' party posed a more serious threat than did the patriarch, with his merely-this-worldly power. The immense construction that follows begins with the definition of a heretic or apostate, Ben Zoma, and then proceeds to a full repertoire of tales about the apostate par excellence, *Elisha ben Abuyah. Though Elisha ben Abuyah was a distinguished disciple of Rabbi Aqiba, not only did he go over to the Romans but he also gave up the Torah.*

They said: It was a day in the summer solstice, and the earth shook and a rainbow appeared in the cloud. And an echo came forth and said to them: Behold the place is vacant for you and the dining couches laid out for you. You and your disciples are destined for the third heaven.

This corresponds to that which is said: In Your presence there is fullness of joy Psalms 16:11. There are seven classes of righteous in the time to come.

Another time, Rabbi Joshua was walking on the road and Ben Zoma came up opposite him. Joshua greeted him, but he did not reply to him. He said to him: Whence and where, Ben Zoma?

Ben Zoma said to him: I have been speculating on the Work of Creation. Between the upper and the lower waters there is nothing but a hand's breadth. It is said here: hovering Genesis 1:2, and it is said there: As an eagle stirs up its nest [and] hovers over its young Deuteronomy 32:11. Just as the "hovering" spoken of there [is] "almost touching but not quite," so the "hovering" spoken of here is "almost touching but not quite."

Joshua said to his disciples: See, Ben Zoma is outside.

It was only a few days before Ben Zoma departed.

Rabbi Judah bar Pazzi in the name of Rabbi Yose ben Rabbi Judah: Three put forward their teaching [on the subject] before their master—Rabbi Joshua before Rabban Yohanan ben Zakkai, Rabbi Aqiba before Rabbi Joshua, Hananiah ben Hakhinai before Rabbi Aqiba. After that time their knowledge becomes impure [that is, the oral tradition of the Merkabah, the mystic chariot, is no longer reliable].

Four entered the Garden [Paradise]. One cast a look and died. One cast a look and was stricken [with madness]. One cast a look and cut among the shoots. One entered safely and departed safely. Ben Azzai cast a look and was stricken. Of him Scripture says: If you have found honey, eat only enough for you Proverbs 25:16. Ben Zoma cast a look and died. Of him Scripture says: Precious in the sight of the Lord is the death of His saints Psalms 116:15. Aher cast a look and cut among the shoots.

Who is Aher? Elisha ben Abuyah, who slew the masters of the Torah. They say: He used to kill every disciple he saw mastering the Torah. Still more, he used to enter the schoolhouse and when he saw the pupils in the presence of the teacher he would say: What are these doing here? This one should be a mason; this one should be a carpenter; this one should be a fisherman; this one should be a tailor. When [the students] heard this they would leave [the teacher] and go [and become workmen].

Of him Scripture says: Let not your mouth lead you into sin Ecclesiastes 5:5. For he ruined his own [good] deeds. Also at the time of the persecution [the Romans] made [the Jews] carry burdens [on the Sabbath], and the Jews arranged it so that two people should share one load, because of the rule about two people doing one piece of work. Elisha said: Make them carry the loads by themselves.

[The Romans] went and made them carry [the loads] by themselves, but [the Jews] arranged to unload at a marked-off plot in a public thoroughfare [an area which cannot be classified either as private ground or as public ground], so that they might not bring [the loads] out from private to public ground [which is forbidden]. Elisha said: Make them carry bottles. [These would be broken if left lying in a public thoroughfare.]

Rabbi Aqiba entered safely, and departed safely. Of him Scripture says: Draw me after you, let us run Song of Songs 1:4.

Rabbi Meir was sitting teaching in the schoolhouse of Tiberias. Elisha, his master, passed by, riding on a horse on the Sabbath day. They came and said to him: Look, your master is outside.

[Meir] stopped his teaching and went out to him. [Elisha] said to him: What were you expounding today? [Meir] said to him: And the Lord blessed the latter days of Job more than his beginning Job 42:12.

Elisha said to him: With what [verse] did you begin to expound it? [Meir] said to him: And the Lord gave Job twice as much as he had before Job 42:10, for He doubled for him all his wealth.

Elisha said: Alas for the things which are lost and not found [meaning, words of Torah]. Aqiba, your master, did not explain it thus, but: And the Lord blessed the latter days of Job from [that is, because of] his beginning on account of the merit of the commandments ∙nd good deeds which he possessed in his former state.

Elisha said to him: And what else have you been expounding? He said to him: Better is the end of a thing than its beginning Ecclesiastes 7:8.

[Elisha] said to him: How did you begin to expound it? [Meir] said to him: [By comparing it] with a man who begot children in his youth and they died, then in his old age he started again. The end of the matter was better than its beginning. [Also by comparing it] with a man who did business in his youth and made a loss, while in his old age he made a profit. The end of the matter was better than its beginning. [Also by comparing it] with a man who learned Torah in his youth, then forgot it, while in his old age he remembered it [literally, he kept it alive]. The end of the matter was better than its beginning.

[Elisha] said: Alas for the things which are lost and not found! Aqiba, your master, did not explain it thus, but: The end of a thing is better than its beginning so long as it is good *from* its beginning. And so it happened. My father, Abuyah, was one of the important people in Jerusalem. When the day of my circumcision came, he invited all the important people of Jerusalem and sat them down in one house, with Rabbi Eliezer and Rabbi Joshua in another house. When they had eaten and drunk they began stamping their feet and dancing.

Rabbi Eliezer said to Rabbi Joshua: While they are occupying themselves in their way we will occupy ourselves in our way. So they sat down and engaged in the study of Torah, from the Pentateuch to the Prophets, and from the Prophets to the Writings. And fire fell from Heaven and surrounded them.

Abuyah said to them: My masters, have you come to burn my house down around me? They said: God forbid! But we were sitting searching around in the words of the Torah from the Pentateuch to the Prophets, and from the Prophets to the Writings, and the words were as alive as when they were given from Mount Sinai. And the fire shone around us as it shone from Mount Sinai.

And the principle of their giving from Sinai? They were given only by fire [as it is written]: And the mountain burned with fire to the heart of Heaven Deuteronomy 4:11.

Abuyah, my father, said to them: My masters, if this is the power of Torah, I will dedicate this son of mine to it so long as he remains alive.

Because his [original] intention was not pure [literally, not for the sake of Heaven], therefore it was not realized in the case of this man [referring to himself, Elisha].

[Elisha] said to him: And what else have you been expounding? [Meir] said to him: Gold and glass cannot equal it Job 28:17.

[Elisha] said to him: How did you begin to expound it? [Meir] said to him: The words of Torah are hard to acquire like vessels of gold but easy to lose like vessels of glass. Just as vessels of gold and glass, when they are broken, can be repaired and become as they [originally] were, so a scholar who forgets his learning can turn and learn it [again] as at the beginning.

[As they spoke together, they had been traveling. Now Elisha] said to him: You have gone far enough, Meir. Here is the Sabbath limit.

[Meir] said to him: How do you know it? He said to him: From the steps [the hooves] of my horse which I am counting; [the horse] has gone 2,000 cubits.

[Meir] said to him: You have all this wisdom, yet you do not repent! I cannot, [Elisha] said.

Why not? Rabbi Meir said to him. Elisha said: Once I was passing before the Holy of Holies riding upon my horse on the Day of Atonement, which happened to fall on a Sabbath, and I heard an echo coming out of the Holy of Holies saying: Repent, children, except for Elisha ben Abuyah, for he knew my power, yet rebelled against me! [alluding to Jeremiah 3:22].

Why did all this happen to him? Once Elisha was sitting and studying in the plain of Gennesaret and he saw a man climb to the top of a palm tree, take a mother-bird with her young, and descend safely. The following day he saw another man climbing to the top of the palm tree; he took the young birds but released the mother. When he descended a snake bit him and he died. Elisha thought: It is written: If you chance to come upon a bird's nest, in any tree or on the ground, with young ones or eggs, you shall not take the mother with the young; you shall let the mother go, but the young shall you take to yourself; that it may go well with you, and that you may live long Deuteronomy 22:6-7. Where is the welfare of this man, and where is his length of days?

[Elisha] did not know that Rabbi Jacob had explained it before him: That it may go well with you — in the world to come which is wholly good. And that you may live long — in the time which is wholly long.

Some say [Elisha defected] because he saw the tongue of Rabbi Judah the Baker in the mouth of a dog dripping blood. He said: This is the Torah, and this its reward! This is the tongue which was bringing forth words of the Torah as befits them. This is the tongue which labored in the Torah all its days. This is the Torah, and this its reward! It seems as though there is no reward [for righteousness] and no resurrection of the dead.

But some say that when his mother was pregnant with him, she passed by some heathen temples and smelled their particular kind of incense. And that odor pierced her body like the poison of a snake.

Some time later Elisha was sick. They came and told Rabbi Meir: Behold, your master is ill. [Meir] went, intending to visit him, and he found him ill.

He said to him: Will you not repent? He said: If sinners repent, are they accepted?

[Meir] replied: Is it not written thus: You cause a man to repent up to the point when he becomes dust? Psalms 90:3. Up to the time when life is crushed are repentant sinners received.

At that moment, Elisha wept, then he departed [this life] and died. And Rabbi Meir rejoiced in his heart, thinking: My master died whilst repenting.

When they buried [Elisha], fire came down from Heaven and consumed his grave. They came and told Rabbi Meir: Behold, your master's grave has been set on fire.

[Meir] went, intending to visit it, and found it burning. What did he do? He took his long prayer cloak and spread it over the corpse, saying: Pass the night Ruth 3:13. Stay in this world which is like the night. And it shall be in the morning Ruth 3:13. This is the world to come which is all morning. If he will redeem you, well and good; let him redeem you Ruth 3:13 – this is the Holy One, blessed be He, of whom it is written: The Lord is good to all, and His compassion is over all that He has made Psalms 145:9. And if it does not please him to redeem you, then, as the Lord lives, I will redeem you Ruth 3:13.

Then the fire was extinguished.

They said to Rabbi Meir: If they ask you in that world: Who do you intend to visit [first], your father or your master [what will you do]? He said to them: I will visit my master first, and after that, my father.

They said to [Meir]: Will they hearken to your plea [for Elisha]? He said to them: Have we not been taught thus: They may save the casing of the scroll together with the scroll [and] the casing of the phylacteries together with the phylacteries? Mishnah Shabbat 16:1. Elisha Aher will be saved through the merit of his [study of the] Torah.

Some time later, Elisha's daughters went to receive alms from Rabbi. Rabbi decreed saying: Let there be none to extend kindness to him, nor any to pity his fatherless children Psalms 109:12.

They said to him: Rabbi, do not look upon his deeds but on his Torah.

At that moment Rabbi wept and decreed that [Elisha's children] should be provided for. He said: If this is what is achieved by this man who labored in the Torah for the wrong motives, how much more would be achieved by one who labors in it for the right motives [that is, literally, for the sake of Heaven]! —YERUSHALMI HAGIGAH 2:1 V-XI

SAGES AND OTHER HOLY MEN

The last sort of competing authority was an acknowledged holy man who clearly stood outside the circle of master-disciple relationships. The sages did not deny that others, outside of their group, might enjoy supernatural favor and exercise power. But they could not approve of them. The selections below represent two subtypes.

First comes the master of knowledge who is not of the sages' group at all. No one will deny that he knows things. But people may not call upon what he knows.

Second is the smart man who is an out-and-out opponent of the sages, that is, who uses his intelligence to ridicule the Torah. Korah is the prototype of such a person, clever enough to ask destructive or embarrassing questions.

There was a case in which a snake bit Eleazar ben Dama. He came to Jacob of Kefar Sama for healing. Rabbi Ishmael said to [Ben Dama]: You have no right to do so, Ben Dama.

[Ben Dama] said to [Ishmael]: I shall bring proof that it is permitted for him to heal me.

But [Ben Dama] did not suffice to bring proof before Ben Dama dropped dead. Rabbi Ishmael said to him: Happy are you, O Ben Dama, for you left this world in peace and did not break through the fence of sages, and so in dying you have carried out that which has been said: A serpent will bite him who breaks through a wall Ecclesiastes 10:8.

And did not a snake already bite him? But a snake will not bite him in the age to come.

And what did [Ben Dama] have to say [in reply to the prohibition against going to Jacob for healing]? You shall therefore keep My statutes and My ordinances, by doing which a man shall live Leviticus 18:5. —YERUSHALMI SHABBAT 14:4 I

Rab said: Korah was an Epicurean. What did he do? He went and made a prayer-shawl which was entirely purple [although the law is that only the fringe was to be purple]. He went to Moses, saying to him: Moses, our rabbi: A prayer-shawl which is entirely purple, what is the law as to its being required to [have] show-fringes?

[Moses] said to him: It is required, for it is written: You shall make yourself tassels [on the four corners of your cloak with which you cover yourself] Deuteronomy 22:12.

[Korah continued:] A house which is entirely filled with holy books, what is the law as to its requiring a *mezuzah* [containing sacred scripture, on the doorpost]?

[Moses] said to him: It requires a *mezuzah*, for it is written: And you shall write them on the doorposts of your house and upon your gates Deuteronomy 6:9.

He said to him: A bright spot the size of a bean — what is the law [as to whether it is a sign of uncleanness in line with Leviticus 13:2ff.]? [Moses] said to him: It is a sign of uncleanness.

[Korah added:] And if it spread over the whole of the man's body? [Moses] said to him: It is a sign of cleanness.

At that moment Korah said: The Torah does not come from Heaven, Moses is no prophet, and Aaron is not a high priest.

Then did Moses say: Lord of all worlds, if from Creation the earth was formed with a mouth, well and good, and if not, then make it now! But if the Lord creates [something new, and the ground opens its mouth, and swallows them up, with all that belongs to them, and they go down alive into Sheol, then you shall know that these men have despised the Lord] Numbers 16:30. — YERUSHALMI SANHEDRIN 10:1 VII

Finally, we deal with a more benign, but still threatening sort of holy man — a miracle-worker favored by Heaven but clearly no sage.

On account of every sort of public trouble (may it not happen) do they sound the shofar, except for an excess of rain. They said to Honi, the circle-drawer: Pray for rain.

He said to them: Go and take in the clay ovens used for Passover, so that they not soften [in the rain which is coming].

He prayed, but it did not rain. What did he do? He drew a circle and stood in the middle of it and said before Him: Lord of the world! Your children have turned to me, for before You I am like a member of the family. I swear by Your great Name—I'm simply not moving from here until you take pity on Your children!

It began to rain drop by drop. He said: This is not what I wanted, but rain for filling up cisterns, pits, and caverns.

It began to rain violently. He said: This is not what I wanted, but rain of goodwill, blessing, and graciousness.

Now it rained the right way, until Israelites had to flee from Jerusalem up to the Temple mount because of the rain. Now they came and said to him: Just as you prayed for it to rain, now pray for it to go away.

He said to them: Go, see whether the stone of the lost has disappeared Mishnah Hagigah 3:9.

Rabbi Yonah, Simeon bar Ba in the name of Rabbi Yohanan [with reference to the final words of the verse: Bring the whole tithe into the storehouse ... that there shall be more than sufficiency Malachi 3:10]: A matter for which it is impossible for you to say, "Enough,"—that is a blessing. [If, however, you can say, "Enough,"—that is no real blessing.]

Rabbi Berekhiah, Rabbi Helbo, Rabbi Abba bar Ilai in the name of Rab: [More than sufficiency] means: Until your lips get tired of saying: Enough blessing! Enough blessing!

[**Go and take in the clay ovens ...**,] that is to say that the incident took place on the eve of Passover. And so it has been taught: On the fourteenth of Nisan all the people prayed for rain and it came.

Now pray for it to go away: [Why did the rain not come properly?] Said Rabbi Yose ben Rabbi Bun: Because [Honi] did not come before God with humility.

Said Rabbi Yudan Giria: This Honi the Circle-drawer was the grandson of Honi and Circle-drawer. He lived near the time of the destruction of the Temple. He went out to a mountain to his workers. Before he got there, it rained. He went into a cave. Once he sat down there, he got sleepy and fell asleep. He remained asleep for seventy years, until the Temple was destroyed and it was rebuilt a second time.

At the end of the seventy years he awoke from his sleep. He went out of the cave, and he saw a world completely changed. An area that had been planted with vineyards now produced olives, and an area planted in olives now produced grain. He asked the people: What do you hear in the world?

They said to him: And don't you know what the news is? He said to them: No.

They said to him: Who are you? He said to them: Honi, the Circle-drawer.

They said to him: We heard that when he would go into the Temple courtyard, he would illuminate it.

[Honi] went in and illuminated the place, and recited concerning himself the following verse of Scripture: When the Lord restored the fortune of Zion, we were like those who dream Psalms 126:1.

It began to rain drop by drop: They said to him: This rain has come only to release you from your vow. **He said: This is not what I wanted, but rain for filling up cisterns, pits, and caverns.** Samuel taught: It poured out as if from a wineskin. **He said, This is not what I wanted, but rain of goodwill, blessing, and graciousness.**

Now it rained the right way, until Israelites had to flee from Jerusalem up to the Temple mount because of the rain. That implies that the Temple mount was roofed over. And so it has been taught: There was a colonnade within the Temple portico. **Now they came and said to him: Just as you prayed for it to rain, now pray for it to go away.**

He said to them: Go, see whether the stone of the lost has disappeared. What purpose did this stone of the lost serve? Whoever lost something would go and find it there, and whoever found something would bring it there. He said: Just as it is not possible for this stone to be blotted out of the world, so it is not possible to pray that rain will go away. But go and bring me a bullock for a thank-offering.

They went and brought him a bullock for a thank-offering. He put his two hands on it and said: Lord [of the ages]! You have brought evil upon Your children, and they could not endure it. You brought good upon Your children, and they could not endure it. But may it be pleasing to You to bring goodness.

Forthwith the wind blew, the clouds were scattered, the sun shone, and the earth dried out. They went out and found the wilderness full of mushrooms.

They asked Rabbi Eleazar: When do they pray that rain should go away? He said to them: If a man is standing on Qeren Ofel [a high rock] and splashes his foot in the Qidron brook. [Then] we shall pray that the rain will stop. Truly it is certain that the Omnipresent will never again bring a flood to the world, for it is said: There will never again be a flood Genesis 9:11. And it says: For this is like the days of Noah to Me: as I swore that the waters of Noah should no more go over the earth, so I have sworn that I will not be angry with you and will not rebuke you Isaiah 54:9. —Tosefta Taanit 2:13 —YERUSHALMI HAGIGAH 3:9 I-IX

9

Our Sages, God, and Torah

POLITICAL POWER GAINED IN THE interstices of a third-rank local authority's administration hardly defined our sages' view of what their sort of man could actually do. They imagined for themselves a quite different power, one that proved paramount in the affairs of nature and nations alike. In the arena of their choosing, they were the only gladiators. And they could tame the wild beasts. Where they struggled, Israel's salvific history and destiny would be decided. How? In examining how they represented their power — the things they could do in this world, the source of their strength — we shall see the answer.

The rule of Heaven and the learning and authority of the rabbi on earth were identified with one another. So salvation for Israel depended upon adherence to the sage and acceptance of his discipline. God's will in Heaven, and the sage's words on earth — both constituted Torah. And since Israel would be saved through Torah, the sage was the savior.

The framers of the Yerushalmi regarded Torah as the source and guarantor of salvation. What they understood by the word "Torah" took on meanings particular to the rabbis. They took to heart as salvific acts what others, standing outside of the sages' social and mythic framework, will have regarded as merely routine, on the one side, or hocus-pocus, on the other. For as we have seen already, to the rabbis the principal salvific deed was to "study Torah." This meant memorizing Torah-sayings by constant repetition, and, as the Talmud itself amply testifies, (for some sages) profound analytic inquiry into the meaning of those sayings.

This act of "study of Torah" imparted supernatural power. For example, by repeating words of Torah, the sage could ward off the angel of death and accomplish other miracles as well. So Torah-formulas served as incantations. Mastery of Torah transformed the man who engaged in Torah-learning into a supernatural figure, able to do things ordinary folk could not do. In the nature of things, the category of "Torah" was vastly expanded, so that the symbol of Torah, a Torah-scroll, could be compared to a man of Torah, namely, a rabbi.

Once it was established that salvation would come from keeping God's will in general, as Israelite holy men had insisted for so many years, it was a small step for rabbis to identify their particular corpus of learning—the Mishnah and associated sayings—with God's will expressed in Scripture, the universally acknowledged revelation. In consequence "Torah," as sages used the term, included, in addition to Scripture, pretty much whatever rabbis knew.

Especially striking in the rabbinical doctrine of salvation is the blurring of boundaries between the nation and the individual. Suffering affected both. Catastrophe of a historical and one-time event, such as the destruction of the Temple, was brought into juxtaposition with personal suffering and death. Accordingly, while the things from which the nation and its people must be saved were many, the mode of salvation was one.

The consequence for the theory of salvation was this: Torah might protect a person from suffering or death, and Torah might in due course save Israel from its subjugation to the nations of the world. In regard to both the individual and society, Torah would save Israel for a life of Torah in Heaven as much as on earth. So we see the sage in a variety of roles, helping the individual and the nation alike.

Since Heaven was conceived in the model of earth, so that the analysis of traditions on earth corresponded to the discovery of the principles of Creation, the full realization of the teachings of Torah on earth, in the life of Israel, would transform Israel into a replica of Heaven on earth. This is, therefore, a doctrine of salvation in which the operative symbol—Torah—and the determinative deed—Torah-learning—defined not only how to reach salvation but also the very nature of the salvation to be attained. The system was whole and cogent. Entering it at any point, one finds the structure as a whole. It is important, then, to recognize that the profound issues confronting Israelite existence, national and individual alike, were framed in terms of Torah and resolved through the medium of Torah. Stated simply: salvation was to come from Torah; the nature of salvation was defined in Torah.

TORAH AND DEATH

The theory of salvation focused upon the Torah addressed the circumstance of the individual as much as of the nation. This was possible because a common factor—sin—had caused the condition of both. Not doing the will of God led to the fall of Israel, the destruction of the Temple. Disobedience to the will of God—that is, sin—is what causes people to suffer and die. The angel of death has power, specifically, over those not engaged in the study of Torah and performance of commandments. That view is expressed in stories indicating the belief that while a sage is repeating Torah-sayings, the angel of death cannot approach him.

[Proving that while one is studying Torah, the angel of death cannot touch him, the following is told:] A disciple of Rabbi Hisda fell sick. He sent two disciples to him, to repeat Mishnah-traditions with him. [The angel of death] turned himself before them into the figure of a snake, and they stopped repeating traditions, and [the sick disciple] died.

A disciple of Bar Pedaiah fell ill. He sent to him two disciples to repeat Mishnah-traditions with him. [The angel of death] turned himself before them into a kind of star, and they stopped repeating Mishnah-traditions, and he died. —YERUSHALMI MOED QATAN 3:4 XXI

TORAH AND CREATION

Since the Torah explained how the world was created, our sages took for granted that adequate knowledge of the Torah would provide them with the key to Creation. The world was made with words, words with letters — so they began speculation about the meaning of letters not yet formed into words, a kind of alphabet-mysticism.

Rabbi Yonah said in the name of Rabbi Levi: The world was created by the letter **B** [the first letter of the Torah]. As **B** [in Hebrew] is closed on all sides except one, so you have no authority to investigate what is above, what below, what went before or shall happen afterwards, only what has happened since the world and its inhabitants were created. If the letter **B** was asked: Who created you? it would point with its upperstroke and say: He above. [If asked:] What is His name? it would point with its lower projection to the right [in the alphabet] and say: YHWH is His name, ADON is His name.

Another interpretation: Why [was the world created] by the letter **B**? Because it is in the word *blessing*. Not by the letter **A**? Because it is in the word for cursing. The Holy One, blessed be He, said: I created My world only by the letter **B** lest its inhabitants should say: How can a world created by the word *cursing* endure? But, behold, I create it by the letter **B** in the word *blessing*, and perhaps it will endure.

Rabbi Abbahu in the name of Rabbi Yohanan: By two letters were the two worlds [this world and the world to come] created. One [was created] by **H** and the other by **Y**. What is the reason? Trust in the Lord for ever, for the Lord God is an everlasting rock Isaiah 26:4. [Rock is here read as "to fashion."] We do not know which was created by **H** and which by **Y**, except from that which is written: These are the generations of the heavens and the earth when they were created. In the day that the Lord God made the earth and the heavens Genesis 2:4. By **H** He created them. This world was created by **H** and the next by **Y**. As **H** is open beneath, this indicates to all the inhabitants of the world that they shall go down to Sheol. As **H** has an upward projection, after they have gone down [to Sheol] they shall go up [to Heaven]. As **H** is open on every side, so a door is open to all who repent. As **Y** is bent, so all the inhabitants of the world shall be bent: Ask now, and see, can a man bear a child? Why then do I see every man with his hands on his loins like a woman in labor? Why has every face turned pale? Jeremiah 30:6.

When David realized [literally, saw] this, he began to praise with the two letters: Praise, O servants of the Lord, praise the name of the Lord Psalms 113:1.

Rabbi Yudan Nesia asked Rabbi Samuel bar Nahum: Why is it written: By means of His name [YAH] lift up a song to Him who rides on the clouds, and exult before Him? Psalms 68:4. He said to him: There is no place which has not an officer [supervising] its entrance. And who is the officer [supervising] the entry of all? The Holy One, blessed be He, for YAH is His name.

[Samuel] said to him: Rabbi Eleazar, your master, did not interpret it thus, but [he compared it] to a king who built a palace in a place of pipes, dunghills, and garbage heaps. Whoever comes and says: This palace is in a place of pipes, dunghills, and garbage heaps – does he not make it seem contemptible? So whoever says: In the beginning the world was water upon water – makes it seem contemptible. [He also compared it] to a king's garden with an upper room built over it. One may look at it, but not touch it. – YERUSHALMI HAGIGAH 2:1 XVI

SAGES AND THE TORAH

The single most important issue is the relationship of the sage to the Torah, and the first of the two principal assertions was that the rulings of the sages stood within the same framework as the rulings found in the written Scriptures. The most important and definitive doctrine of the Yerushalmi and the whole of the canon of which it forms a chief component is what is here asserted.

[As at Mishnah Sanhedrin 11:4] associates in the name of Rabbi Yohanan: [Leiden MS and *editio princeps*: Rabbi:] **The words of scribes are more beloved than the words of Torah and more cherished than words of Torah[, as it is written]:** Your palate is like the best wine Song of Songs 7:9.

Simeon bar Ba in the name of Rabbi Yohanan: The words of scribes are more beloved than the words of Torah and more cherished than words of Torah: For your love is better than wine Song of Songs 1:2.

Rabbi Ba bar Kohen in the name of Bar Pazzi: You should know that the words of scribes are more beloved than the words of Torah. For lo, as to Rabbi Tarfon[, to whom Mishnah Berakhot 1:3 refers as follows: Said Rabbi Tarfon: I was coming along the way, and I inclined to recite the Shema, in accord with the opinion of the House of Shammai, and I endangered myself because of bandits. They said to him: You deserved to be subject to such liability, because you transgressed the words of the House of Hillel], had he [merely] not recited the Shema, he would have violated only a positive commandment [of the Torah, to recite the Shema morning and night]. But because he transgressed the words of the House of Hillel, he turned out to be liable to the death penalty. This was by reason of the following verse: A serpent will bite him who breaks through a wall Ecclesiastes 10:8.

Rabbi Ishmael repeated the following: The words of Torah are subject to prohibition, and they are subject to remission; they are subject to lenient rulings, and they are subject to strict rulings. But words of scribes all are subject only to strict interpretation, for we have learned there: **He who rules: There is no requirement to wear phylacteries—in order to transgress the teachings of the Torah, is exempt. But if he said: There are five partitions in the phylactery, instead of four—in order to add to what the scribes have taught, he is liable** Mishnah Sanhedrin 11:3.

Rabbi Hanina in the name of Rabbi Idi in the name of Rabbi Tanhum ben Rabbi Hiyya: More stringent are the words of the elders than the words of the prophets. For it is written: Do not preach Micah 2:6 – thus they preach – one should not preach of such things. And it is written: [If a man should go about and utter wind and lies, saying:] I will preach to you of wine and strong drink – he would be the preacher for this people! Micah 2:11.

A prophet and an elder – to what are they comparable? To a king who sent two of his senators to a certain province. Concerning one of them, he wrote: If he does not show you my seal and signet, do not believe him. But concerning the other one, he wrote:

Even though he does not show you my seal and my signet, believe him. So in the case of the prophet, He has had to write: If a prophet arises among you ... and gives you a sign or a wonder.... Deuteronomy 13:1. But here [with regard to an elder]: ... according to the instructions which they give you.... Deuteronomy 17:11 [without a sign or a wonder]. —YERUSHALMI ABODAH ZARAH 2:7 [Leiden MS and *editio princeps: 2:8*]

THE SAGE AS TORAH

The theological position that the teaching of sages, or scribes, falls into the category of divine revelation or Torah comes to concrete expression in the mythic view that the person of the sage is comparable to the physical object, the Torah scroll. The sage is a living and breathing Torah. That view is expressed in numerous concrete and material ways. Since, as we have seen, God is understood wholly within anthropomorphic terms, we should hardly be surprised that people see as human (that is, the anthropomorphization of) the Torah scroll as well. The claim that a sage (or a disciple of a sage) was equivalent to a scroll of the Torah produces a material, legal comparison, not merely a symbolic metaphor. This is the meaning of the first two excerpts below.

Rabbi Jacob bar Abayye in the name of Rabbi Aha: An elder who forgot his learning because of some accident which happened to him—they treat him with the sanctity owed to an ark [of the Torah]. —YERUSHALMI MOED QATAN 3:1 XI

He who sees a disciple of a sage who has died is as if he sees a scroll of the Torah that has been burned. —YERUSHALMI MOED QATAN 3:7 X

In the last extract, the master enjoys the forms of respect reserved for the Torah.

Said Rabbi Eleazar: The Torah does not stand up before her son [the master]. Samuel said: One does not stand before an associate.

Rabbi Hila [and] Rabbi Jacob bar Idi were in session. Samuel bar Ba passed by, and they rose before him. [Samuel] said to [them]: There are two errors you have now committed. First, I am not an elder, and second, the Torah does not stand up before her son. [When you are studying Torah, you need not interrupt to stand up before a master.]

Said Rabbi Zeira: Rabbi Aha would interrupt his study and rise. For he takes account of the following teaching, which has been taught: Those who write scrolls [of the Torah], phylacteries, and *mezuzot* interrupt their work to say the *Shema,* but they do not do so to say the Prayer.

Rabbi Hanania ben Aqabiah says: Just as they interrupt their labor to recite the Shema, so they interrupt it to say the Prayer, to put on phylacteries, and for various other religious duties enjoined by the Torah.

When Hezekiah ben Rabbi was tired of his labor in learning in the Torah, having completed his task, he would go and sit down before the schoolhouse, so that he would see elders and rise before them.

Judah bar Hiyya made a practice of going up and asking after the welfare of Rabbi Yannai. He would see him from one Friday to the next, and would set himself down in a given place, so that he would see him and so have to rise up before him. His disciples said to him: Did you not teach us, Rabbi, that for an elder, one remains standing until he passes for four cubits? He said to them: There is no question of sitting down before *Sinai.*

On one occasion he did not go up. [Yannai] said: It is not possible that Judah, my son, should change his normal custom. He said: It is not possible that some sort of suffering has come on the person of that righteous man [for he will not suffer]. Hence it is likely that we no longer have Judah ben Rabbi with us.

Rabbi Meir maintained that even in the case of an old man who was ignorant, one should rise before him. He said: It is not for nothing that he has lived a long time. [He must have some other merit than learning.]

Rabbi Hanina would hit anyone who did not rise before him, saying to him: Do you want to nullify the Torah?

Said Rabbi Simon: Said the Holy One, blessed be He: You shall rise up before the hoary head, and honor the face of an old man, and you shall fear your God; I am the Lord Leviticus 19:32. I am the one who first carried out the requirement of standing before an elder.

When the patriarch enters, everybody stands before him, and it is not permitted for any of them to sit down, until he says to them: Be seated. When the head of the court enters, they set up rows [of disciples] before him. If he wants, he passes through this row, and if he wants, he passes through that one. When a sage enters, one stands and the one before sits down, one stands and the one before sits down, until he reaches his place and sits down.

When Rabbi Meir would come to teach, he would go up to the meeting-house, and everyone would gaze at him and rise before him. When they heard this teaching [about how a sage is treated], they wanted to treat him in this way, [and] he grew angry and walked out. He said to them: I heard that one raises the level of sanctification, but one does not lower the level of sanctification.
—YERUSHALMI BIKKURIM 3:3 V

THE SAGE
AND THE PROPHET

To the extent the ancient Israelite prophets could foretell the future, the sage also told told stories about various ways in which sages could predict things that were going to happen. The basis of the prediction — knowledge of Torah, supernatural instruction through echoes from Heaven — does not change the fact that the sage claimed to exercise precisely the validating powers of the prophet of old. So the sage was a prophet.

Said Rabbi Eleazar: They follow what is reported by the sound of an echo. What is the scriptural basis for this view? And your ears shall hear a word behind you, saying: This is the way, walk in it, when you turn to the right or when you turn to the left Isaiah 30:21.

Rabbi Eleazar went to a privy and sat down. A Roman quartermaster came along and made him get up and sat down in his place. [Eleazar] said to himself: No one in the world did he push aside except for me. It is not possible for me to leave here until I find out what it is all about.

There was a snake in the privy, and it came out and bit [the Roman] on his anus. [Eleazar] recited in his own regard: Because you are precious in My eyes, and honored, and I love you, I give men in return for you, peoples in exchange for your life Isaiah 43:4.

A disciple of Bar Qappara was going out to cut logs. A field worker saw a snake running after him and said to him: A snake is running after you. The snake left off pursuing the disciple and went after the [worker], and the disciple recited in his own regard: [Because you are precious in My eyes, and honored, and I love you,] I give men in return for you [, peoples in exchange for your life].

Germania, a slave of Rabbi Judah the Patriarch, went out and wanted to lend money to Rabbi Hila. A mad dog came along and wanted to snap at Rabbi Hila. Germania shouted at the dog, and it left off Rabbi Hila and ran after him, and [Hila] recited in his own regard: [Because you are precious in My eyes, and honored, and I love you,] I give men in return for you [, peoples in exchange for your life].

Bar Qappara went into a certain town. As he came in, he stubbed his toe. He got up and heard the voice of children reciting this verse: If he comes in single, he shall go out single; if he comes in married, then his wife shall go out with him Exodus 21:3. He said: It seems to me I will accomplish nothing here except for this contusion — and that is just what happened.

Rabbi Yohanan and Rabbi Simeon ben Laqish wanted to go see Samuel [in Babylonia]. They said: We shall follow the counsel of an echo. They passed by a class and heard the voice of the students: Now Samuel died; and all Israel assembled and mourned for him, and they buried him in his house at Ramah. Then David rose and went down to the wilderness of Paran 1 Samuel 25:1. They took that as an omen, and that is just what had happened.

Rabbi Yonah and Rabbi Yose went up to visit Rabbi Aha, who was failing. They said: We shall follow the counsel of an echo. They heard a woman saying to her friend: Has the light gone out? The other said to her: The light has not gone out, and the light of Israel will not go out. [They took this as a sign that he would recover, and he did.]

Rabbi Yohanan was passing through the marketplace, and he saw a man selling sweets. He said to him: Do you make a living from these? He said to him: Yes. He left him and went away. A while later he came by again. The man said to him: Rabbi, pray for me, for from the time you went by, I have not sold a thing. He said to him: Move somewhere else, for sometimes changing your name brings luck, and sometimes changing your location does.

Two disciples of Rabbi Hanina were going out to cut wood. They saw an astrologer. He said: These two will go out but not come back. When they went out, an old man met them and said to them: Acquire merit by helping me, for I have gone three days without tasting any food. [The disciples] had with them a single circle of figs which they divided and half of which they gave to him. He ate it and prayed for them. He said to them: May you live out this day, just as you have helped me to live out this day. They went forth whole and came back whole. There were present people who had heard the report [of the astrologer's [prediction]. They said [to the astrologer]: Now did you not say to us that these two would go out and not come back? He said: There is a liar in this spot, for his [my] astrological science has fooled me. Even so, they went and looked into the bundles [the disciples] were bearing, and they found a snake cut in half, one part in the knapsack of one of them, one part in that of the other. They said to the disciples: Now what sort of thing did you do today? They repeated the story. [The astrologer] said: Now what can I do, when the God of the Jews is appeased by a half-circle of figs!

Rabbi Huna reports the following story: A certain astrologer converted to Judaism. One time he wanted to go out [on a trip]. He said: Is this the right time to go out? Then he retracted and said: Now did I not cleave unto this holy people in order to leave off these sorts of things? Let us call on the name of our Creator. When he came near a dangerous place [where there was a wild beast], he gave bread to the beast, and it ate the bread [instead of the astrologer]. What made him fall into danger? That he had fallen into doubt. And what saved him? That he had relied on his Creator.

He said to him: Whoever foretells the future — in the end [what he predicts] will come upon him. What is the scriptural basis for this statement? For there is no enchantment against Jacob, no divination against Israel; now it shall be said of Jacob and Israel: What has God wrought! Numbers 23:23. For to him [who practices enchantment] will the enchantment [come]. —YERUSHALMI SHABBAT 6:9 I

THE SAGES AS INTERPRETERS OF DREAMS

It was not a long step from predicting the future on the basis of messages delivered from the supernatural world or knowledge of the Torah to interpreting dreams and their meaning, as seen in the two examples that follow.

A certain person once came before Rabbi Yose ben Halafta. He said to him: I had a dream in which I was told: Go to Cappadocia and you will find some of your father's belongings. [Rabbi Yose] said to him: Did your father ever go to Cappadocia during his lifetime? He responded: No. Rabbi Yose said to him: Go and count to the twentieth beam in your house and you will find your father's belongings – [for the Cappadocia in your dreams denotes] *Kappa dokia* [Greek for "twenty beams"].

A certain person once came before Rabbi Yose ben Halafta. He said to him: I saw in my dream [that I was told]: Put on a crown of olive branches. [Rabbi Yose] said to him: You will be exalted at the end of days. Another person came to him and said: I saw in my dream [that I was told]: Put on a crown of olive branches. [Rabbi Yose] said to him: You will be flogged. He asked Rabbi Yose: Why did you tell him he will be exalted and you told me I will be flogged [and yet we both had the same dream]? Rabbi Yose responded: That person [saw olives when they were just] in blossom [and would grow more splendid, but your olives were ripe and] ready to be beaten [for their oil].

A certain person came to Rabbi Ishmael ben Rabbi Yose. He said to him: I saw in my dream [that I saw] one watering an olive tree with oil. [Rabbi Ishmael] said to him: You will die for you have slept with your mother.

A certain person came to Rabbi Ishmael ben Rabbi Yose. He said to him: I saw in my dream [that I saw] one of my eyes watering its fellow. [Rabbi Ishmael] said to him: You will die for you have slept with your sister.

A certain person came to Rabbi Ishmael ben Rabbi Yose. He said to him: I saw in my dream [that] I had three eyes. [Rabbi Ishmael] said to him: You will make an oven. Two of the eyes are yours and one is the eye [that is, the ventilation hole] of the oven.

A certain person came to Rabbi Ishmael ben Rabbi Yose. He said to him: I saw in my dream [that I had] four ears. [Rabbi Ishmael] said to him: You will fill up [a vat of wine]. Two of the ears are yours and two are the ears [that is, the handles] of the vat.

A certain person came to Rabbi Ishmael ben Rabbi Yose. He said to him: I saw in my dream [that] people fled before me. [Rabbi Ishmael] said to him: You will bring a prickly twig and all the people will fall before you.

A certain person came to Rabbi Ishmael ben Rabbi Yose. He said to him: I had a dream [in which I was told]: Cover yourself with a codex of twelve leaves! [Rabbi Ishmael] said to him: Your blanket has twelve patches.

A certain person came to Rabbi Ishmael ben Rabbi Yose. He said to him: I had a dream [in which I was told]: Swallow a star. [Rabbi Ishmael] said to him: You will die, for you have killed Jews. [The star represents Jews, as it is said:] A star came forth from Jacob Numbers 24:17 [that is, the star represents the descendants of Jacob].

A certain person came to Rabbi Ishmael ben Rabbi Yose. He said to him: I saw in my dream [that] my vineyard gave forth lettuce. [Rabbi Ishmael] said to him: Your wine will come out so sweet that you will take lettuce and dip it in the wine's vinegar. [Even vinegar made from the grapes will be so sweet you will use it as a condiment.]

A certain person came to Rabbi Ishmael ben Rabbi Yose. He said to him: I saw in my dream [that] I was told: Thus did your finger throw down. [Rabbi Ishmael] said to him: Give me my fee and I will tell you [what this means].

He said to him: I saw in my dream [that] I was told: Thus shall it swell in your mouth. [Rabbi Ishmael] said to him: Give me my fee and I will tell you [what this means].

He said to him: I saw in my dream [that I was told]: Thus shall your finger be straight.

[Rabbi Ishmael] said to him: Did I not say: Give me my fee and I will tell you its meaning? When you were told: Thus did it throw down, [this meant you will wipe] drippings from your wheat. When you were told: Thus [shall it swell in your mouth, this meant that the wheat] has become swollen. And when you were told: Thus [shall your finger be straight, this meant that the wheat] is sprouting.

A certain Samaritan said: I shall go and outwit that elder of the Jews [by fabricating a dream and asking him to interpret it]. He went to [Rabbi Ishmael] and said to him: I saw in a dream four cedars and four sycamores, a bundle of reeds, a skin, [and] cows, and I was sitting and stamping. [Rabbi Ishmael] said to him: May you die, for this was not a dream. Even so you shall not leave empty-handed. The four cedars are the four posts of a bed. The four sycamore trees are the four legs of a bed. The bundle of reeds is the footboard. The skin is the range on which the straw [lies]. The cows are the fingers [that is, the cross slats of the bed frame that support the mattress]. And the man sitting and stamping is a man lying on it neither alive nor dead [but incurably ill]. And thus did it happen to that [Samaritan. He was bedridden with a long, painful disease.]

There was once a woman who came to Rabbi Eliezer. She said to him: I saw in my dream [that] the second [beam] of my house was broken. He said to her: You will give birth to a son. She went and gave birth to a son.

A few days later she came to consult him [again]. His students said to her: He is not here. They said to her: What do you want from him? She said to them: I saw in my dream [that] the second beam of my house was broken. They said to her: You will give birth to a son, but your husband will die.

When Rabbi Eliezer came, they recounted the episode. He said to them: You have killed someone! How? Because a dream is always fulfilled according to the interpretation given it, as it is said: And as he interpreted it for us, so was it Genesis 41:15. [That is, had the students not told the woman that her husband would die, he would still be alive.]

Said Rabbi Yohanan: All dreams are fulfilled according to their interpretation except for [dreams one has after drinking] wine.

There are some who drink wine and it is good for them, and there are some who drink wine and it is bad for them. A disciple of the sages drinks wine and it is good for him. An *am ha'ares* drinks wine and it is bad for him.

A certain person came to Rabbi Aqiba. He said to him: I saw in my dream [that] one of my legs was shorter than the other. [Aqiba] said to him: When the festival comes, you will not eat meat. [That is, the leg in the dream [RGL] is taken to be a symbol for a pilgrimage festival [RGL]. Just as the leg is lacking something, so too will the holiday.]

Another came to [Aqiba] and said to him: I saw in my dream [that] my leg was overly large. [Aqiba] said to him: When the festival comes, you will have a lot of meat.

One of Rabbi Aqiba's students was sitting there and was upset. [Aqiba] said to him: What is the matter? He said to him: I heard in my dream three distressing sayings: You will die in [the month of] Adar ['DR], In [the month of] Nisan [NYSN] you will not see, and Whatever you plant you will not gather in. [Aqiba] said to him: These three [sayings] are good. [You simply have interpreted them incorrectly.] [The first means] that you will be exalted in the glory [HDR'] of the Torah. [The second means] that you will not experience trials [NYSYN]. [And the third, which says:] Whatever you plant you will not gather in, [means that the children] you have begotten, you will not bury. —YERUSHALMI MAASER SHENI 4:9 III [Translated by Peter Haas]

10

Our Sages, God, and Israel

IN THE TORAH, THE SAGE HELD in his hand the power to bring salvation not only to individuals but also to all Israel. The Torah as taught by the sage was the source not simply of immediate and personal redemption but of Israel's salvation. The supernatural power imputed to the sage was a foretaste of what would come when all Israel conformed to the Torah as the sage taught it. So tales of the supernatural or magical power of the rabbi must be read in the context of the larger setting of the salvific process posited by the Talmud's framers. What was the theory behind the identification of our sages' supernatural or magical power with Israel's ultimate, historical redemption?

It was an axiom of all forms of Judaism that because Israel had sinned, it was punished by being given over into the hands of earthly empires; when Israel atoned, it was, and again would be, removed from their power. The means of atonement, reconciliation with God, were specified elsewhere as study of Torah, practice of commandments, and performance of good deeds. Why so? The answer is distinctive to the matrix of the Yerushalmi: When Jews in general had mastered the Torah as rabbis embodied it, they would become rabbis, just as some now were rabbis, saints, and holy men.

When all Jews had become rabbis, they would no longer lie within the power of other nations, that is, of history. Then the Messiah would come. Redemption, then, depended upon all Israel's accepting the yoke of the Torah. At that point all Israel would attain a full and complete embodiment of Torah – that is, revelation. Thus conforming to God's will and replicating Heaven, Israel on earth – as a righteous, holy community – would exercise the supernatural power of Torah. They would then be able as a whole to do what some few saintly rabbis could do at present. With access to supernatural power, redemption would naturally follow.

The clearest picture of the theory of salvation contained within the Judaism attested by the Talmud of the Land of Israel is to be found in the sages' reading of Scripture. Specifically, the worldview projected by them upon the heroes of ancient Israel clearly reveals the sages' view of the salvation of themselves and their world. Ancient modes of salvation would work again. The Talmud's framers naturally took for granted that the world they knew in the fourth century had flourished a thousand and more years earlier. The values they embodied and the supernatural powers they fantasized for themselves predictably were projected backward onto biblical figures. The ubiquitous citation of biblical prooftexts in support of both legal and technological statements shows the mentality of the Talmud's framers. In their imagination, everything they said stood in direct continuity with Scripture. Biblical and Talmudic authorities lived on a single plane of being, in a single age of shared discourse; the Mishnah and associated documents amply restated propositions held for all time and proved in Scripture, too. What is important is the theory of salvation given its clearest statement in the sages' reading of the ancient salvific record.

What was the rabbis' view of salvation? Seeing Scripture in their own model, they took the position that the Torah of old, with its supernatural power and salvific promise, continued to endure in their own day, among themselves. In consequence, the promise of salvation contained in every line of Scripture was to be kept in every deed of learning and obedience to the law effected under their auspices. In an act of (to us) extraordinary anachronism they projected backward the things they cherished, while (in their eyes) they carried forward, to their own time, the promise of salvation for Israel contained within the written Torah of old.

GOD JUDGES ISRAEL

The first point in the salvific doctrine is simply that God judges Israel. And God judges Israel with mercy.

There we learned: **Lo, whoever sits and does not commit a transgression—they pay him a reward like that of him who performs a commandment.**

Said Rabbi Zeira: This speaks of someone who had the opportunity to do something which might or might not be a transgression, and who did not do it.

Said Rabbi Yose ben Rabbi Bun: This speaks of someone who designated for himself a given religious duty and never in his life transgressed it.

What would be examples of such a thing?

Said Rabbi Mar Uqban: For example, honoring father and mother. Said Rabbi Mana: **Blessed are those whose way is blameless, who walk in the law of the Lord** Psalms 119:1. [They are] like those who walk in the law of the Lord. Said Rabbi Abun: **Who also do no wrong, but walk in His ways** Psalms 119:3. It is as if they walk in His ways.

Rabbi Yose ben Rabbi Bun [said]: What is the meaning of the following verse of Scripture: **Blessed is the man who walks not in the counsel of the wicked?** Psalms 1:1. Since he did not walk in the counsel of the wicked, it is as if he walked in the counsel of the righteous.

Ben Azzai interpreted the following verse: **Dead flies make the perfumer's ointment give off an evil odor** Ecclesiastes 10:1. Now will a single dead fly not make the perfumer's ointment give off an evil odor? [Of course it will.] Now this one, because he did a single sin, he lost all the merit which was in his possession.

So did Rabbi Aqiba interpret the following verse: **Therefore Sheol has enlarged its appetite and opened its mouth beyond measure** Isaiah 5:14. **Beyond measures** is not written here, but rather **beyond measure.** This may be compared to a person who did not have in his hand a single religious duty to incline the balance in his favor.

That which you say applies to the world to come. But as to this world, even if nine hundred and ninety-nine angels argue against him and a single angel argues for him, the Holy One, blessed be He, inclines the balance in his favor. And what is the scriptural basis for that statement? If there be for him an angel, a mediator, one of the thousand, to declare to man what is right for him, and He is gracious to him, and says: Deliver him from going down into the pit, I have found a ransom Job 33:23-24.

Said Rabbi Yohanan: If you hear a teaching of Rabbi Eliezer, son of Rabbi Yose the Galilean, incline your ear like a water clock and listen carefully.

For Rabbi Yohanan said: Rabbi Eliezer, son of Rabbi Yose the Galilean, says: Even if nine hundred and ninety-nine angels argue against a person, and a single angel argues in his favor, the Holy One, blessed be He, inclines the scales in his favor. And that is not the end of the matter as to that angel. For even if nine hundred and ninety-nine aspects of the argument of that single angel argue against a man, and but a single aspect of the case of that single angel argues in favor, the Holy One, blessed be He, still inclines the scales in favor of the accused. What is the scriptural basis for that statement? If there be for him an angel one of the thousand [M'LP] is not written, but rather one part of the thousand [MNY 'LP] meaning one thousandth of the aspects of the arguments of that single angel.

What is written immediately following? And He is gracious to him, and says: Deliver him from going down into the pit, I have found a ransom. Deliver him—through the atonement of suffering. I have found a ransom—he has found a ransom for himself.

That which you have said applies in this world, but as to the world to come, if the man has a larger measure of merits, he inherits the Garden of Eden, and if he has a larger measure of transgressions, he inherits Gehenna.

If they were equally balanced? Rabbi Yose ben Hanina said: ... forgiving sin ... Micah 7:18. Rabbi Abbahu said: It is written: ... forgiving ... What does the Holy One, blessed be He, do? He snatches one of his bad deeds, so that his good deeds outweigh the balance. —YERUSHALMI QIDDUSHIN 1:9 II

ISRAEL'S GOOD QUALITIES

Given the long list of complaints drawn up by our sages against their Israelite constituency, we should expect the prophetic tradition of social criticism to find its counterpart. But the following story reveals that our sages took for granted traits in Israel that we must regard with considerable admiration. The story is not directly concerned with Israel's good qualities, a fact that makes all the more stunning the narrator's routine assumptions about how Jews act. Jews might be punished for idolatry, fornication, and murder. But they are identified as a people commonly characterized by modesty, kindness, and caring — the opposite of sinful deeds. So, in judging Israel, God (like David) must balance the routine against the extraordinary, punishing the latter but inclining the scale through the weight of the former.

Now there was a famine in the days of David for three years; [and David sought the face of the Lord] 2 Samuel 21:1. Said David: It is on account of three things that rain will be held back: idolatry, fornication, and murder.

Idolatry, as it is written: Take heed lest your heart be deceived, and you turn aside and serve other gods and worship them Deuteronomy 11:16, and adjacent to this verse: And the anger of the Lord be kindled against you, and He shut up the heavens, so that there be no rain Deuteronomy 11:17.

Fornication, as it is written: Therefore the showers have been withheld, and the spring rain has not come; yet you have a harlot's brow Jeremiah 3:3.

Murder, as it is written: For blood pollutes the land Numbers 35:33.

And there are those who say: Also one who publicly pledges to give to charity but fails to carry out his pledge, as it is written: Like clouds and wind without rain is a man who boasts of a gift he does not give Proverbs 25:14.

Now [in seeking the reason for the drought and famine], David made inquiry into all his doings, and he did not find any reason. He addressed his question to the Urim and Thummim. This is in line with that which is written: And David sought the face of the Lord.

Said Rabbi Eleazar: It is written: Seek the Lord, all you humble of the land, who do His commands Zephaniah 2:3. And the Lord said: There is bloodguilt on account of Saul and on his house, because he put the Gibeonites to death 2 Samuel 21:1. On account of Saul – because you did not bury him properly. And on account of the bloodguilt on his house – because he put the Gibeonites to death.

So David sent and called [the Gibeonites] and said to them: What is between you and the house of Saul? They said to him: It is because he killed seven of us, two hewers of wood, two drawers of water, a scribe, a teacher, and a beadle.

He said to them: And what do you want now? They said to him: Let seven of his sons be given to us, so that we may hang them up before the Lord at Gibeon on the mountain of the Lord 2 Samuel 21:6.

He said to them: Now what pleasure do you have if you kill them? Take silver and gold for yourselves. They said to him: We don't want anything to do with silver and gold from Saul and his house. He said: Perhaps some of [the Gibeonites] are ashamed before others to accept such a ransom.

So [David] took each one of them and tried to win him over by himself, but none of them went along with him. This is in line with the following verse of Scripture: It is not a matter of silver and gold between us and Saul or his house 2 Samuel 21:4. . . . Between *me* [individually] . . . – it is written.

At that moment, David said: The Holy One, blessed be He, gave to Israel three good qualities: modesty, kindness, and caring.

Modesty, as it is said: And Moses said to the people: Do not fear; for God has come to prove you, and that the fear of Him may be before your eyes, that you may not sin Exodus 20:20.

Kindness, as it is written: . . . so that He will show you mercy, and have compassion on you, and multiply you, as He swore to your fathers Deuteronomy 13:7.

Caring, as it is said: Know therefore that the Lord your God is God, the faithful God who keeps covenant and steadfast love. . . . Deuteronomy 7:9.

Now these [Gibeonites], by contrast, do not exhibit any of these traits. So he set them afar from the Israelites. Now the Gibeonites were not of the people of Israel 2 Samuel 21:2. —YERUSHALMI SANHEDRIN 6:7 II

THE COMMANDMENTS

Through carrying out God's commandments, Jews do routinely what is in fact remarkable. In this way, they express that humanity of theirs that is in God's image and likeness. Doing the commandments means to do what God does, to imitate God. Here is how the Yerushalmi describes carrying out commandments affecting family life, what parents owe children and what children owe parents.

What is **a commandment pertaining to the father concerning the son**? Mishnah Qiddushin 1:7. To circumcise him, to redeem him, and to teach him Torah, and to teach him a trade, and to marry him off to a girl. And Rabbi Aqiba says: Also to teach him how to swim Tosefta Qiddushin 1:11.

To circumcise him, in line with the following verse of Scripture: And on the eighth day the flesh of his foreskin shall be circumcised Leviticus 12:3.

To redeem him, in line with the following verse of Scripture: Every first-born of man among your sons you shall redeem Exodus 13:13.

To teach him Torah, in line with the following verse of Scripture: And you shall teach them to your children [talking of them when you are sitting in your house, and when you are walking by the way, and when you lie down, and when you rise] Deuteronomy 11:19.

To teach him a trade: Rabbi Ishmael taught: [I call Heaven and earth to witness against you this day, that I have set before you life and death, blessing and curse;] therefore choose life [that you and your descendants may live] Deuteronomy 30:19. This [refers to] learning a trade.

To marry him off to a girl, in line with the following verse of Scripture: [Only take heed, and keep your soul diligently, lest you forget the things which your eyes have seen, and lest they depart from your heart all the days of your life;] and make them known to your children and your children's children Deuteronomy 4:9. Under what circumstances do you have the merit [of seeing] children and grandchildren? When you marry your children off when they are young.

Rabbi Aqiba says: Also to teach him how to swim, in line
with the following verse of Scripture: [I call Heaven and earth to
witness against you this day, that I have set before you life and
death, blessing and curse; therefore choose life] that you and
your descendants may live. —YERUSHALMI QIDDUSHIN 1:7 I

How far does the requirement of honoring the father and
mother extend? [Eleazar] said to them: Are you asking me? Go and
ask Damah ben Netinah. He was the chief of the council of elders
of his town. One time his mother was slapping him before the entire
council, and the slipper with which she was beating him fell from
her hand, and he got down and gave it back to her, so that she would
not be upset.

Said Rabbi Hezekiah: He was a gentile from Ashkelon, and
head of the council of his town. Now if there was a stone on which
his father had sat, he would never sit on it. When [his father] died,
he made the stone into his god.

One time the Benjamin's jewel in the high priest's breastplate
was lost. They said: Who has one as fine as that one? They said that
Damah ben Netinah had one. They went to him and made a deal
with him to buy it for a hundred *denars.* He went to get it for them,
and found that his father was sleeping [on the box containing the
jewel]. And some say that the key to the box was on the finger of
his father, and some say that his foot was stretched out over the
jewel-cask.

[Damah] went down to them and said: I can't bring it to you.
They said: Perhaps it is because he wants more money. They raised
the price to two hundred, then to a thousand.

Once his father woke up from his sleep, [Damah] went up
and got the jewel for them. They wanted to pay him what they had
offered at the end, but he would not accept the money from them.
He said: Shall I sell you [at a price] the honor which I pay to my
father? I shall not derive benefit by reason of the honor which I pay
to my father.

How did the Holy One, blessed be He, reward him? Said
Rabbi Yose ben Rabbi Bun: That very night his cow produced a red
cow, and the Israelites paid him its weight in gold and weighed it

[to use it for producing purification-water in line with Numbers 19:11ff.]. Said Rabbi Shabbetai: It is written: [The Almighty—we cannot find Him; He is great in power and justice,] and abundant righteousness He will not violate Job 37:23. The Holy One, blessed be He, will not long delay the reward which is coming to the gentiles for the good that they do.

The mother of Rabbi Tarfon went down to take a walk in her courtyard on the Sabbath, and her slipper fell off, and Rabbi Tarfon went and placed his two hands under the soles of her feet, so that she could walk on them until she got to her couch. One time sages went to call on [Tarfon]. [His mother] said to them: Pray for Tarfon, my son, who pays me altogether too much honor. They said to her: What does he do for you? She repeated the story to them. They said to her: Even if he did a thousand times more than this, he still would not have paid even half of the honor of which the Torah has spoken.

The mother of Rabbi Ishmael went and complained to the rabbis about him. She said: Rebuke Ishmael, my son, because he does not pay respect to me. At that moment the faces of our rabbis grew dark. They said: Is it at all possible that Rabbi Ishmael does not pay honor to his parents?

They said to her: What did he do to you? She said: When he comes home from the council house, I want to wash his feet in water and drink the water, and he does not allow me to do it.

They said: Since that is what she deems to be the honor she wants for herself, that indeed is just the kind of honor he must pay to her. Said Rabbi Mana: Well do the millers say: Everyone's merit is in his own basket. [That is, there is a different way of doing good for every person.] The mother of Rabbi Tarfon said one thing to them, and they responded thus, and the mother of Rabbi Ishmael said something else to them, and they responded so.

Rabbi Zeira was distressed, saying: Would that I had a father and a mother, whom I might honor, and so inherit the Garden of Eden. When he heard these two teachings [about Tarfon and Ishmael], he said: Blessed be the All-Merciful, that I have no father and mother. I could not behave either like Rabbi Tarfon or like Rabbi Ishmael.

Said Rabbi Abin: I am exempt from the requirement of honoring father and mother. They say that when his mother became pregnant, his father died, and when his mother gave birth, she died.

There is one who feeds his father fattened [birds] and inherits Gehenna, and there is one who ties his father to the millstones [to pull them] and inherits the Garden of Eden.

How does one feed his father fattened [birds] and inherit Gehenna? There was a man who gave his father fattened chickens to eat. One time the father said to him: My son, how do you come by these things? He said to him: Old man, eat and shut up, just like dogs that eat and shut up. So he turns out to feed his father fattened [birds] and yet inherits Gehenna.

How does one tie his father to the millstones and inherit the Garden of Eden? There was a man who was a miller, pulling the stones. The government orders came to the millers [for the corvee]. He said to him: Father, go and pull the wheel in my place. If the [labor for the government] should be dishonorable, it is better that I do it and not you, and if there should be floggings, it is better that I receive them and not you. So he turns out to tie his father to the millstones and yet inherits the Garden of Eden.

Every one of you shall revere his mother and his father [and you shall keep My sabbaths] Leviticus 19:3. And it is said: You shall fear the Lord your God; [you shall serve Him and swear by His name] Deuteronomy 6:13. Scripture thus compares the reverence owing to father and mother to the reverence owing to the Omnipresent.

It is said: Whoever curses his father or his mother shall be put to death Exodus 21:17. And it is said: [And say to the people of Israel:] Whoever curses his God shall bear his sin Leviticus 25:15. Scripture thus compares the penalty for cursing the father and mother to the penalty for cursing the Omnipresent.

But it is not possible to introduce the matter of smiting Heaven.

But these [comparisons] are reasonable, for the three of them are partners. —YERUSHALMI QIDDUSHIN 1:7 VI

RABBI DAVID, KING-MESSIAH

The people Israel thus accepts God's will and seeks through obedience to the Torah to make itself into God's likeness and image. How then will the people be saved? It will be through the Messiah, the anointed one chosen by God to save Israel. And what sort of person will the Messiah be? In the nature of things, we should not be surprised that it will be a man, and a sage, a rabbi like all other rabbis. At the same time, of course, everyone knew the biblical traditions that pointed toward David's eternal household as the Messiah's ancestry. Accordingly, the Messiah will come from David and the Messiah will be a rabbi, and, it must follow, to understand the character and identification of the Messiah, we have to look to David himself.

If David, king of Israel, was like a rabbi of the sages' day, then a rabbi of the sages' day would be the figure of the son of David, who was to come as king of Israel. It is not surprising, therefore, that among the many biblical heroes whom the talmudic rabbis treated as sages, principal and foremost was David, now made into a messianic rabbi or a rabbinical Messiah. He was the sage of the Torah, the avatar and model for the sages of their own time. That view was made explicit, both specifically and in general terms. If a rabbi was jealous to have his traditions cited in his own name, it was because that was David's explicit view as well. In more general terms, both David and Moses are represented as students of Torah, just like the disciples and sages of the Yerushalmi's time.

[The following refers to 2 Samuel 23:15-16: And David longed and said: O that someone would give me water to drink from the well of Bethlehem which is by the gate! And the three mighty men broke through the host of the Philistines, and drew water out of the well of Bethlehem that was by the gate. Now water here is understood to mean *learning*, gate is understood as the rabbinical court, and David is thus understood to be asking for instruction. At issue is the battlefield in which the Philistines had hidden themselves, that is, as at Pas-dammim. What troubled David is under discussion.]

David found it quite obvious that he might destroy the field of grain and [so he would have to] pay its cost [DMYM].

Could it be obvious to him that he might destroy the field and *not* pay its cost [to its Israelite owners]? [It is not permissible to rescue oneself by destroying someone else's property, unless one pays compensation. So that cannot be at issue at all.]

[If he did have to pay, as he realized, then what he wanted to know at the gate was] which of them to destroy, and for which of the two he should pay compensation [since he did not wish to destroy both the fields which Rabbi Samuel posited were there]. [The choice then was] between the field of lentils and the field of barley.

The one of lentils is food for man, and the one of barley is food for beast. The one of lentils is not subject, when turned into flour, to a dough-offering, and the one of barley is subject, when turned into flour, to dough-offering. As to lentils, the *omer* is not taken therefrom; as to barley the *omer* is taken therefrom. [So these are the choices before David, and since there were two fields, he wanted to know which to burn and for which to pay compensation.]

—YERUSHALMI SANHEDRIN 2:5 III

THE RABBI AS
THE SAVIOR OF ISRAEL

Just how a rabbi serves to save Israel is illustrated in tales told (we may assume, by the patriarch's staff) about Judah the Patriarch, author of the Mishnah and ethnarch of Israel in the land of Israel. In the following stories, the storytellers project onto the figure of the patriarch-sage all of those messianic tasks that can be done in this world and at this time. He saves Israel through his suffering. He protects Israel by his merits. He rules Israel justly and with gentleness. Bearing the title "Rabbi" by itself, Judah the Patriarch thus figures, in these tales, as the prototype of the rabbi-messiah or rabbi-savior whom our sages promised for the future.

The Yerushalmi effects an astonishing parallelism between Scripture and sage. In a word, the Talmud constructs the rabbi as Scripture incarnate, therefore (completing the trilogy) the hope and salvation of Israel. Out of the union of the Torah and the person of the rabbi, the messianic and salvific faith, rabbinic Judaism, was born. Judah the Patriarch thus stands for the system as a whole.

What the rabbis of the Yerushalmi bequeathed to Israel and the West, in the end, is a vision of man in the image of God, a model for what a man can be: not mud alone but mind as well. This legacy served to exalt man's unique powers of thought, to order his daily routine and endow it with a wonderful sense of its formal perfection. So the national-historical life of Israel was matched by and joined to the local and private life of the village. The whole served as a paradigm of ultimate perfection — sanctification; hence, salvation. The power of the Yerushalmi's vision endures for an age with a lesser view of humanity. Ours is a diminished faith in the human capacity of rationality to attain orderly rules for sanctification in the everyday and so to gain salvation in the end of days.

The Sepphoreans said: Whoever tells us that Rabbi has died shall we kill.

Bar Qappara approached them, with his head covered, and his clothing torn. [He said to them:] The angels and the mortals had laid hold of the tablets, and the angels got the upper hand and have seized the tablets.

They said to him: Rabbi has died. He said to them: You have said so.

Then they tore their clothes, and the noise of their tearing of their clothes reached Papa, three *mils* away.

Rabbi Nathan in the name of Rabbi Mana [said]: There were miracles done that day. It was the eve of the Sabbath, and all the villagers assembled to make a lamentation for him. En route to burial, they put down the bier eighteen times to mourn him, and they accompanied him down to Bet Shearim. The daylight was protracted until each one of them had reached his home [in time for the Sabbath] and had time to fill up a jug of water and to light the Sabbath lamp. When the sun set, the cock crowed, and the people began to be troubled, saying: Perhaps we have violated the Sabbath.

But an echo came to them: Whoever did not refrain from participation in the lamentations for Rabbi may be given the good news that he is going to enjoy a portion in the world to come, except for the launderer [who used to come to Rabbi day by day, but did not bother to participate in his funeral].

When [the launderer] heard this, he went up to the roof and threw himself down and died. Then an echo went forth and said: Even the laundryman [will enjoy the life of the world to come].

Rabbi lived in Sepphoris seventeen years, and he cited the following verse in his own regard: And Jacob lived in the land of Egypt seventeen years; [so the days of Jacob, the years of his life, were a hundred and forty-seven years] Genesis 47:28. Thus: And Judah lived in Sepphoris for seventeen years, and of that time he spent thirteen years suffering from a toothache.

Said Rabbi Yose ben Rabbi Bun: During that entire period of thirteen years, a woman in labor never died in the Land of Israel, nor was there ever a miscarriage in the Land of Israel.

And why did [Rabbi] suffer from pain in the teeth? One time he was passing by and saw a calf being taken to the slaughter. It lowed in terror, but Rabbi said to it: Go, for this is the purpose for which you were created.

And in the end [when the pain was made to cease] how was [Rabbi] healed? [Rabbi] saw how they were killing a nest of mice, and he said to them: Let them be. It is written: [The Lord is good to all,] and His compassion is over all that He has made Psalms 145:9.
—YERUSHALMI KETUBOT 12:3 IV

IMAGES OF HUMANITY: PROMETHEUS OR ADAM?

We end where we began, with Adam, the first human being, and the Yerushalmi's images of this hermaphroditic precursor. These naturally portray Adam's Creator as well. What is expressed are concerns for God and God's love for humanity, the absolute bedrock of the Yerushalmi's conception of humanity. The following excerpt is the counterpart to the myth in which Prometheus angered the deity by making fire. By contrast, in the Yerushalmi God showed love to humanity by bestowing the gift of fire. God created human beings out of love, protects and cherishes us since we are made "In Our Image, after Our Likeness," and, in the fullness and end of time, will save us. This is the Yerushalmi's image of humanity. All that we are and do serves to praise God, in whose image we are created, and to whose glory we give evidence. That is who we are. Such was the gift and vision of our sages, defying their circumstances — and ours as well.

Rabbi Levi in the name of Rabbi Nezira [said]: For thirty-six hours that light which was created on the first day served [the world] — twelve on the eve of the Sabbath [Friday], twelve on the night of the Sabbath, and twelve on the Sabbath. And the first man [Adam] looked at it from one end of the world to the other. When the light did not cease [from shining], the whole world began to sing, as it is said: Under the whole Heaven, He lets [His voice] go, and His light to the corners of the earth Job 37:3.

When the Sabbath ended, it began to grow dark. Man became frightened, saying: This is the one concerning whom it is written: He will bruise your head, and you shall bruise his heel Genesis 3:15. Perhaps this one has come to bite me. And he said: Let only darkness cover me Psalms 139:11.

Rabbi Levi said: At that moment the Holy One, blessed be He, prepared two flints and struck them against each other, and the light came forth from them. This is the meaning of that which Scripture says: And the light around me be night Psalms 139:11. And he [man] blessed it, thanking God *Who creates the light of the fire.*
—YERUSHALMI BERAKHOT 8:5

Index

Passages Cited

BIBLE

Psalms

5:12, *8*	72:18-19, *12*	109:12, *129*
16:11, *124*	89:8, *6*	113:1, *139*
18:14, *60*	89:33, *51*	115:8, *32*
18:51, *54*	90:3, *129*	116:15, *125*
31:20, *8*	91:15, *47*	119:1, *153*
32:6, *8*	92:15, *110*	119:3, *153*
36:7, *69*	94:23, *12*	126:1, *133*
41:2, *70*	97:7, *32*	127:1, *70*
48:15, *61*	106:30, *40*	139:11, *165*
50:3, *5*	106:44, *56*	145:9, *129, 164*
58:6, *35*	106:45, *56*	146:5, *31*
60:12, *15, 17*	106:46, *56*	146:6, *31*
68:4, *139*		

Ruth

3:13, *129*

1 Samuel

2:23-51, *121*	2:28, *36*	6:19, *20*
2:27, *42*	3:1, *61*	25:1, *144*

2 Samuel

7:23, *121*	21:2, *156*	21:6, *156*
Ch. 20, *85*	21:4, *156*	23:15-16, *161*
21:1, *155-156*		

Song of Songs

1:2, *140*	6:2, *3*	7:9, *139*
1:4, *126*		

Zechariah

3:2, *19*	9:13, *42*	11:17, *16*

Zephaniah

2:3, *156*

MISHNAH

Abodah Zarah

2:1, *25*	3:1, *30*	4:7, *31*

Abot

3:1, *2*

Baba Mesia

2:11, *105-106*

Baba Qamma

4:3, *25*

Index II
Subjects and Names